THE HUMAN RIGHT TO DEVELOPMENT
IN A GLOBALIZED WORLD

This book is dedicated to my parents
Kevin and Pauline Aguirre

The Human Right to Development in a Globalized World

DANIEL AGUIRRE

Routledge
Taylor & Francis Group

LONDON AND NEW YORK

First published 2008 by Ashgate Publishing

Published 2016 by Routledge
2 Park Square, Milton Park, Abingdon, Oxon OX14 4RN
711 Third Avenue, New York, NY 10017, USA

Routledge is an imprint of the Taylor & Francis Group, an informa business

British Library Cataloguing in Publication Data
Aguirre, Daniel
   The human right to development in a globalized world
   1. Human rights 2. Globalization 3. Economic development
   I. Title
   303.4'4

Library of Congress Cataloging-in-Publication Data
Aguirre, Daniel.
   The human right to development in a globalized world / by Daniel Aguirre.
     p. cm.
   Includes bibliographical references and index.
   ISBN 978-0-7546-7471-9
   1. Economic development. 2. Globalization--Economic aspects. 3. Human rights. I.
Title.

   HD75.A37 2008
   338.9--dc22

2008018467

Transfered to Digital Printing in 2011

ISBN 9780754674719 (hbk)

Contents

Acknowledgements

There are many friends and colleagues that I would like to acknowledge for their assistance and support during the course of my research. Firstly, I would like to thank the Irish Centre for Human Rights and the National University of Ireland for providing an amicable venue for research and learning. I extend my gratitude to Prof. Joshua Castellino, Dr Kathleen Kavanaugh, Dr Vinodh Jaichand, Dr Raymand Murphy and the rest of the staff for all their fine work. In particular, I wish to thank Prof. William A. Schabas for his invaluable insight. Thanks also to Bruce Porter and Prof. Koen De Feyter for their comments, advice and ideas. In addition, Dr David Keane and Irene Pietropaoli provided important editing and helpful advice. I wish also to tip my hat to all those who granted me unwavering friendship in Galway and Port Elgin, Ontario. Your support was essential to this long process. Finally, I wish to thank my parents, to whom this book is dedicated.

Chapter 1

Introduction: Economic Globalization and Human Rights

One of the most profound challenges that we face as a community of nations is to understand better the emerging socio-economic forces and forms of globalization, to shape them to serve our needs and to respond effectively to their deleterious consequences.[1]

The effects of globalization are resonating around the world. Developments in technology, communications and transportation have facilitated a rapid increase in transnational political, economic and social exchanges. This has affected international relations and relations between states and multinational corporations.[2] Economic globalization is associated with economic interdependence, deregulation and a dominance of a liberalized marketplace. Globalization is touted as the basis of rapid development. But economic globalization has only strengthened international networks of trade and investment[3] creating highly interdependent regions.[4]

Since the end of the Cold War, the international political economy has experienced fundamental changes.[5] Cold War alliances once dominated the world economy as well as development policy. Thus markets were subjugated to political and economic security. Liberal values were not prioritized. Since then, competition between states has significantly increased. Developing states have been brought into, and now actively participate in, this competitive market-orientated international system.

Economic globalization now dominates international relations.[6] Development strategy consists of liberal trading regimes with a reduced role for the state. International relations now involve states, the market, multinational corporations

1   Annan, K. (1998), *Partnerships for a Global Community: Annual Report on the Work of the Organization, 1998* (UN Sales No. E.99.I.3, New York).

2   Steiner, H. and Alston, P. (2000), *International Human Rights Law in Context* (2nd edn, Oxford University Press), 940.

3   Koenig-Archibugi, M. (2003), 'Introduction: Globalization and the Challenge of Governance', in Held, D. and Koenig-Archibugi, M. (eds), *Taming Globalization: Frontiers of Governance* (Cambridge: Polity Press), 2.

4   Rugman, A. (2001), *The End of Globalisation* (New York: American Management Association, AMACOM), 3-4.

5   See Gilpin R. (1987), *The Political Economy of International Relations* (Princeton University Press).

6   Gilpin, R. (2001), *Global Political Economy: Understanding the International Economic Order* (Princeton University Press), 18.

and international organizations.[7] This globalization may make the task of fulfilling non-market goals at the national level more difficult. Specifically, the realization of the right to development, based on principles of economic self determination and global solidarity, may be impeded.[8]

International investment is a prominent component of economic globalization. Investment's focus on profit-maximization and competitiveness can contradict the fulfillment of human rights entitlements.[9] In a resolution on the question of the impact of globalization and its effect on human rights, the United Nations General Assembly recognizes that: 'while globalization offers great opportunities, the fact that its benefits are very unevenly shared and its costs unevenly distributed represents an aspect of the process that affects the full enjoyment of all human rights, in particular in developing countries'.[10]

Economic globalization has increased the number and influence of multinational corporations, nearly all of which are based in G7 states.[11] Of the top 500, only 29 are from low income states.[12] Companies incorporated in the United States dominate the important industrial, financial and service industries.[13] Of the world's 100 largest economic entities, 51 are now corporations and 49 are countries.[14] It is estimated that in 1970, there were 7,000 corporations. In 1993 there were 37,000 corporations, and by 2003, 64,000 with 870,000 foreign subsidiaries.[15] The largest 500 corporations control 70 per cent of global trade and are the primary international investors. As a result of this expansion, corporate interests dominate economic globalization and influence the policy of individual states.[16]

The investment operations of corporations, the regulatory role of the state, and the right to development are the subject of this book. What began as research into the inadequacy of human rights law pertaining to economic globalization became

7   *Ibid.*

8   Declaration on the Right to Development (4 Dec 1986), UNGA Res. 41/128, annex 41, Supp. No. 53 at 186, UN Doc. A/41/53 (DRD).

9   The United Nations General Assembly has called globalization 'not merely an economic process but [one that] has social, political, environmental, cultural and legal dimensions which have an impact on the full enjoyment of all human rights'. See UNGA, 'Globalization and its Impact on the Full Enjoyment of All Human Rights' (14 Dec 2000), UN Doc. A/RES/55/102 para.2; see also UNGA, 'Globalization and its Impact on the Full Enjoyment of All Human Rights' (17 Dec 1999), UN Doc. A/RES/54/165, para.2.

10   UNGA, 'Globalization and its impact on the full enjoyment of all human rights' (16 Dec 2005), UN Doc. A/RES/60/152, para.5.

11   See United Nations Conference on Trade and Development (1994), *World Investment Report 1994: Transnational Corporations, Employment and the Workplace* (New York).

12   Monbiot, G. (2003), *The Age of Consent: A Manifesto for a New World Order* (London: Flamingo), 195.

13   Goldstein, J. (2003), *International Relations* (5th edn, New York: Longman), 367.

14   Anderson, S. and Cavanagh, J., 'Top 200: The Rise of Corporate Global Power' (Institute for Policy Studies, published online 4 Dec 2000) <http://www.corpwatch.org/article.php?id=377>, accessed 10 March 2008.

15   'A Taxing Battle', *The Economist* (31 January 2004), 66.

16   Buckman, G. (2005), *Global Trade: Past Mistakes, Future Choices* (Zed Books), 95.

a study on the unwillingness of states to fulfill their human rights obligations both domestically and internationally. After all, as Olivier de Schutter observes:

> ... what may appear in a static analysis as a disempowerment of the states confronted with a new form of sovereignty competing with theirs is, it should be remembered, the result of the emergence of a global marketplace which is initially the creation of the states. Less than ever should we exculpate states from their alleged inability to tame the new leviathans.[17]

Economic globalization can produce the capital needed to provide for human rights. Human rights law can help to contain the detrimental social effects of globalization. Human rights can balance market forces within a just international political framework.[18] The ability and willingness of states to discharge their human rights obligations is crucial to this system. The United Nations General Assembly emphasizes that: 'While globalization, by its impact on, inter alia, the role of the state, may affect human rights, the promotion and protection of all human rights is first and foremost the responsibility of the state.'[19] It is put forward here that the Declaration on the Right to Development sets out a national and global framework of responsibility for states to do so.

Globalization entrenches trade liberalization and market expansion. The establishment of the World Trade Organization through the Uruguay Round of the General Agreement on Tariffs and Trade solidified this regime.[20] The Uruguay round created a legal framework for liberalization in trade-related aspects of intellectual property[21] and trade in services.[22] This increased the enforcement powers of the regime through the establishment of a sophisticated dispute settlement process.[23] Centralized international planning and decision making, for example via the United Nations, is no longer possible in the economic sphere.

The issue of trade and human rights has become a central concern.[24] Recent human rights discourse has been devoted to the study of multinational corporations and their direct effect on human rights.[25] Yet, the foundation of globalization – the state's

---

17   De Schutter, O. (2005), 'The Accountability of Multinationals for Human Rights Violations in European Law', in Alston, P. (ed.), *Non-State Actors and Human Rights* (Oxford University Press), 314.

18   Koenig-Archibugi, M., *supra* n. 3, 1.

19   UNGA, 'Globalization and its impact on the full enjoyment of all human rights' (16 Dec 2005), UN Doc. A/RES/60/152, para.1.

20   Marrakech Agreement Establishing the World Trade Organization (15 April 1994), LT/UR/A/2.

21   Agreement on Trade-Related Aspects of Intellectual Property Rights (15 April 1994), LT/UR/A-1C/IP/1.

22   General Agreement on Trade in Services (15 April 1994), LT/UR/A-1B/S/1.

23   Understanding on Rules and Procedures Governing the Settlement of Disputes (15 April 1994), LT/UR/A-2/DS/U/1.

24   Orford, A. (2003), 'Globalization and the Right to Development', in Alston P. (ed.), *Peoples' Rights* (Oxford University Press), 166-67.

25   See Addo, M. (ed.) (1999), *Human Rights Standards and the Responsibility of Transnational Corporations* (The Hague: Kluwer Law International); Kamminga, M. and Zia-

political, legal and economic facilitation of foreign investment by corporations.has not been subjected to analysis in human rights terms. The human rights must now be achieved in a global economy that prioritizes investment protection.

Market based economic theory presupposes perfect competition and the free functioning of international markets. However, investment is conducted under oligopolistic conditions in imperfect markets that afford the investor, often a developed world corporation, unique opportunities for the exploitation of global resources. Corporations are encouraged to utilize market imperfections and influence political relations with host-states.[26] The promotion of their interests pushes corporations to extend control over foreign economies and influence the regime governing competition.[27] Thus, the protection afforded corporations by investment treaties is central to the relationship between states. Even political alliances depend on the treatment of corporations.[28]

The negative effects of corporations on human rights in development can be divided into two categories. First, the corporation may directly violate human rights by itself or in conjunction with another actor. This typically involves civil and political rights, such as the right to personal security. For example, a corporation may hire state security forces to protect its facilities that engage in torture as occurred in Myanmar in association with Unocal Corp.[29] Also, a corporation may directly violate rights by prohibiting collective bargaining or discriminating against minorities. The second category concerns indirect effects. This involves the corporation's influence on host governments. Corporations can undermine the state's ability to fulfill human rights law. They use their influence to encourage governments to adopt policies of liberalization, deregulation and privatization that ignore human rights consequences.

This second effect concerns mostly economic, social and cultural rights, which are vital in developing states. Corporations are the engines of economic growth upon which states depend for the provision of the right to development. Increasingly, corporations are more economically powerful and influential than the developing host-states from which they extract their profits. These states seem unable, without

Zarifi, S. (eds) (2000), *Liability of Multinational Corporations under International Law* (The Hague: Kluwer Law International); Stephens, B. (2002), 'Stefan A. Riesenfeld Symposium 2001: The Amorality of Profit: Transnational Corporations and Human Rights', *Berkeley Journal of International Law* 20, 45.

26   See Korten, R. (1995), *When Corporations Rule the World* (West Hartford, CT: Kumarian Press).

27   See Vernon, R. (1971), *Sovereignty at Bay* (New York: Basic Books).

28   Gilpin, R., *supra* n. 6, 18.

29   e.g. *Doe I v. Unocal Cor*, 963 F. Sup880 (C.D. Cal. 1997); *Nat'l Coalition Gov't of the Union of Burma v. Unocal, Inc.*, 176 F.R.D. 329 (C.D. Cal. 1997); *Doe I v. Unocal Cor*, 67 F. Sup2d 1140 (C.D. Cal. 1999); *Doe I v. Unocal Cor*, 110 F. Sup2d 1294 (C.D. Cal. 2000); *Doe I v. Unocal Cor*, 27 F. Sup2d 1174 (C.D. Cal. 1998), *affidavit* 248 F.3d 915 (9th Cir. 2001); see also: International Labour Organization, 'Forced labour in Myanmar (Burma), Report of the Commission of Inquiry appointed under Article 26 of the Constitution of the International Labour Organization to examine the observance by Myanmar of the Forced Labour Convention (2 July 1998), 1930 (No. 29) Parts III.8, V.14 (3); UNGA, 'Situation of Human Rights in Myanmar' (16 Dec 1995), UN Doc. A/RES/50/194 1995.

international cooperation, to fulfill the human rights obligations required to complete the right to development process. International cooperation to curb the negative influence of corporations is not forthcoming as the global economy depends on the expansion of investment.

The human rights regime has been criticized for its state-centric approach that seems out of place in a global economy with diverse powerful actors. State-centrism seems to insulate human rights discourse from vital challenges posed by non-state actors. The traditional approach reinforces the state as the central actor around which everything else revolves.[30] Is the state still the sovereign decision maker that human rights law was designed to regulate?

The questions surrounding international cooperation and the right to development cannot be examined without addressing the role of corporations and the regulation of their investment activities. Corporations are important actors within the process of economic globalization.[31] It is assumed that these non-state actors have reduced ties to their home-states and have become powerful political entities in themselves. This leads to the assumption that they dictate international economic and political affairs. The role and significance of the corporation in domestic and international affairs is a much-debated topic within the field of international political economy.

The multinational corporation is incorporated in a particular state but owns and controls subsidiaries through foreign investment in other states. The purpose of foreign direct investment is to achieve partial or complete control over marketing, production, or other facilities in the services, manufacturing or commodities sectors of another state. Purchasing existing businesses or the construction of new ones, accompanied by mergers, takeovers and alliances with corporations of other states, is all included in foreign direct investment. It is therefore part of an overall corporate strategy to achieve a permanent position within host economies.[32] When this occurs, the home-state's economy benefits.

The corporation has transformed the global economy and some states have lost influence as corporations have become global in nature.[33] This is considered a movement towards a global economy where there will be no national products or economies.[34] Global development strategy reflects this; the corporation is now the

---

30   Alston, P. (2005), 'The "Not-a-Cat" Syndrome: Can the International Human Rights Regime Accommodate Non-State Actors?' in Alston, P. (ed.), *supra* n. 17, 3.

31   See Stopford, J., Henley, J. and Strange, S. (1991), *Rival States, Rival Firms: Competition for World Market Shares* (Cambridge University Press).

32   Despite the frequent reference to the political and economic might of corporations and the foreign investment system this is not a new regime. In the past, the merchant adventurers such as the Dutch East India Company and the Massachusetts Bay Company were far more powerful. These forerunners to the modern corporations commanded their own fleets and armies, conducted foreign policy and controlled territory. See Gilpin, R., *supra* n. 6, 278.

33   For an example of such theory see Ohmae, K. (1990), *The Borderless World: Power and Strategy in the Interlinked Economy* (New York: Harper Business).

34   See generally, Reich, R. (1991), *The Work of Nations: Preparing Ourselves for 21st Century Capitalism* (New York: Knopf).

most important source of capital and technology, having replaced foreign aid in this regard.[35]

But the activities of the corporation still require the consent of states. Consider the following: first, the corporation remains physically headquartered in the home-state; second, empirical studies have shown that corporations still depend on their state of incorporation for sales;[36] third, corporations generally reflects the managerial culture of their home-states; and finally, the corporation is viewed in the host-state as an instrument of the home-state.[37] International political economy discourse still considers the corporation as 'a creature of its home economy'.[38] Perhaps most importantly, they rely on their home-states to bilaterally facilitate investment protection for their activities.

The global expansion of corporations has been promoted by states. States have granted corporations rights through trade agreements, bilateral investment treaties and domestic liberalization.[39] The development of a neoliberal economy and the subsequent reduction of the state have led many observers to predict a shift to a market-driven international economy.[40] Obviously, such a shift would have profound implications for the implementation of an international development policy and human rights law. The state becomes less and less relevant as it encourages a global capitalist market of unrestricted trade, finance and investment.[41]

Although corporations provide valuable investment and capital to states, they depend upon host-states to provide protection and rule of law, well-regulated markets and a stable political environment. It is important to remember that the states themselves construct market imperfections in order to encourage investment.[42] States adopt concessionary policies to attract capital. Tax breaks and favourable investment conditions for foreign firms are common market manipulations of this type.[43] The creation of regional trade blocs and investment treaties reflect the interests of their

35 Gilpin, R., *supra* n. 6, 279.

36 Gestrin, M., Knight, A. and Rugman, A. (2001), *The Templeton Global Performance Index* (Oxford University Press).

37 Saul, J. (2005), *The Collapse of Globalism and the Reinvention of the World* (Penguin), 83.

38 Gilpin, R., *supra* n. 6, 278.

39 See Ruggie, J. (22 Feb 2006), 'Interim Report of the Special Representative of the Secretary-General on the Issue of Human Rights and Transnational Corporations and Other Business Enterprises', UN Doc. E/CN.4/2006/97 para.12.

40 See Strange, S. (1996), *The Retreat of the State: The Diffusion of Power in the World Economy* (Cambridge University Press); Camilleri, J. and Falk, J. (1992), *The End of Sovereignty? The Politics of A Shrinking and Fragmenting World* (Aldershot, UK: Edward Elgar); Van Creveld, M. (1999), *The Rise and Decline of the State* (Cambridge University Press); Ohmae, K. (1995), *The End of the Nation State* (New York: Free Press); Schmidt, V. (1995), 'The New World Order, Incorporated: The Rise of Business and the Decline of the Nation-State' *Daedalus* 75.

41 Strange, S., *supra* n. 40, 9.

42 Gilpin, R., *supra* n. 6, 279.

43 See Krugman, P. and Obstfeld, M. (1994) *International Economics: Theory and Practice* (3rd edn, New York: Harper Collins), 162.

dominant member states.[44] Production and service industries remain nationally based as profit flows back to home-states.[45]

States make the rules for the global economy. Corporations carry out the transactions within these rules. Multinational corporations are merely companies based in one state with branches and subsidiaries and/or investments in other states.[46] They operate on a large scale and simultaneously in many states, in pursuit of profits within the rules of the global economy. They have the potential to support foreign governments that violate human rights law as well as press for important change in those regimes.[47] The relations between states and corporations within the system of foreign investment are of utmost importance to achieving the human right to development.

This book begins to scrutinize investment treaties in light of the right to development. Arbitration under these treaties between developing states and corporations can have a direct impact on human rights. Therefore, it is vital that they are monitored and subjected to human rights-based criticism. New negotiating efforts by states to create more of these investment rules (whether they be bilateral, or regional and multilateral instruments such as the negotiations on the Free Trade Area of the Americas or the actions of the World Trade Organization) must be subjected to scrutiny and analyzed through human rights discourse. If left isolated, the international investment regime may be discredited, lose legitimacy and be subject to political backlash. Worse yet, it may evolve into a system which permanently prevents the realization of the right to development.

Activists, academics and development practitioners in many fields are striving to ascertain how global economic integration influences the human rights project.[48] This book is an interdisciplinary examination of the politics and economics of globalization and their impact on the right to development. Economic globalization and the rise of corporate power has created rapid economic growth but has simultaneously fostered extreme inequality and underdevelopment that can undermine human rights. The international community has failed to regulate economic globalization according to human rights norms. Instead, states have cooperated on a bilateral and regional level to create investment agreements. Globalization based on foreign investment is thus put forward by states as an international developmental system. This system is incongruent with the full realization of human rights, the right to development and the spirit of international cooperation put forward by the Charter of the United Nations and the Universal Declaration of Human Rights.[49]

---

44   Gilpin, R., *supra* n. 6, 297.

45   Sally, R. (1994), 'Multinational Enterprises, Political Economy and Institutional Theory: Domestic Embeddedness in the Context of Internationalization', *Review of International Political Economy* 1.1, 161-92.

46   Goldstein, J., *supra* n. 13, 367.

47   See Goldstein, J., *supra* n. 13, 13; Anghie, A. (1999), 'Finding the Peripheries: Sovereignty and Colonialism in Nineteenth-century International Law', *Harvard International Law Journal* 40, 37.

48   See De Feyter, K. (2005), *Human Rights: Social Justice in the Age of the Market* (Zed Books), 2.

49   Universal Declaration of Human Rights (10 Dec 1948), UNGA Res 217A (III), UN Doc. A/810 at 71 (UDHR).

The rules of international investment caught civil society's attention during the negotiations on the Organization for Economic Cooperation and Development's Multilateral Agreement on Investment in the mid-to-late 1990s. Although the agreement was halted, partly due to rising public concern about the implications of the multilateral agreement on investment upon domestic sovereignty and issues related to human rights, similar investment rules were written into a host of other bilateral and regional treaties. Prominent amongst those is the North American Free Trade Agreement that is a model for hundreds of other agreements.[50] These agreements have an immediate impact on national economies and international relations as they can restrict state policy.[51]

Global economic concepts are often oversimplified and generalized under the term 'global trade'. International investment is a prominent component of globalization and an example of cooperation between states. The interaction of the investment regime with human rights is an unformed area of law. The impact of foreign investment on human rights has been neglected due to the fact that it is conducted by corporations. Foreign investment is not governed by an international institution or an international treaty, such as the World Trade Organization, for example, leaving it to states to deal with bilaterally.

Foreign direct investment consists of a long-term relationship between the home-state (the state of incorporation) and host-state (the state in which the investment is made) of the corporation. The Multilateral Agreement on Investment[52] would have given investors enhanced rights within their host-states automatically. An international system regulating this important dimension of economic globalization has failed to materialize so far. Nevertheless, the proliferation of bilateral and regional negotiations has facilitated increases in foreign direct investment. Bilateral investment treaties purport to be politically neutral and economic in nature, despite their obvious consequences, both positive and negative, for development, governance and human rights.[53]

Bilateral investment protection treaties are contracts between states. States also bear responsibility for upholding human rights law. Investment treaties can prioritize the property rights of foreign investors over many non-market initiatives derived to fulfill positive human rights law obligations.[54] Various investment treaty provisions may prohibit regulations that address market failures in protecting collective goods during development. Investment treaties potentially override the rights-based development process essential for the fulfillment of the right to development.

---

50   Wai, R. (2002), 'Transnational Liftoff and Juridical Touchdown: The Regulatory Function of Private International Law in an Era of Globalization', *Columbia Journal of International Law* 40, 214.

51   Chossudovsky, M. (2003), *The Globalization of Poverty and the New World Order* (2nd edn, Montreal: Global Research), 24.

52   Organization of Economic Cooperation and Development, 'Multilateral Agreement on Investment: Draft Negotiating Text' (24 Apr 1998).

53   Wai, R., *supra* n. 50, 214.

54   Shalankany, A. (2000), 'Arbitration and the Third World: A Plea for Reassessing Bias under the Specter of Neoliberalism', *Harvard International Law Journal* 41, 419.

Bilateral regimes can only work fairly if conducted between states of relatively equal economic development. Otherwise, the reciprocity governing the agreement will be illusory. Bilateral agreements are intended to encourage investment by protecting the basic interests of both the capital importing and exporting state.[55] Yet, at the bilateral level, developed-underdeveloped relations are characterized by dependency. Dependent relationships make it difficult for states to regulate foreign investment in order to address human rights concerns. By contrast, multilateral deals can allow developing states to group together in negotiations with dominant states.[56] An international agreement should contain human rights safeguards and protect the human rights regulatory role of developing states.

The prioritization of investment in global governance appears to dislocate citizens from their entitlements under human rights law.[57] Democracy requires a state to control social and economic conditions within its jurisdiction.[58] Representative debate should reflect the will of the populace on economic regulations.[59] Conflicts of interest can arise between the rights-based approach to development and the investment protection system. The prioritization of investment insulates states from the demands of citizens. The proliferation of these agreements can render states more accountable to foreign investors than to local populations. There is no doubt that such treaties strengthen the position of corporations.[60]

International investment law compels states to enact legislation ensuring domestic enforcement. Under the 1965 Convention on the Settlement of Disputes Between States and Nationals of Other States,[61] corporations have standing in tribunals concerning the terms of investment treaties. These tribunal systems can compromise regulations related to human rights.[62] A number of cases have raised worrying questions about the legitimate sphere of host-state regulation. For example, a fee schedule for health care or education targeted at ensuring equal access and participation would be prohibited as a performance requirement, or as indirect expropriation, both prohibited under investment treaties. Investors could challenge the provision of subsidized public services, affirmative action policies or a public insurance system as indirect expropriation of market opportunity.[63]

---

55 Shaw, M. (2003), *International Law* (5th edn, Cambridge University Press), 747.

56 'The Future of Globalization', *The Economist* (29 July 2006), 11.

57 Shalankany, A., *supra* n. 54, 419.

58 See generally, Held, D. (1995), *Democracy and the Global Order* (Cambridge: Polity Press).

59 Koenig-Archibugi, M., *supra* n. 3, 3.

60 Shalankany, A., *supra* n. 54, 429.

61 The Convention on the Settlement of Disputes between States and Nationals of Other States, 18 March 1965, Reprinted in 4 ILM (1965), 532. For commentary, see Schreuer, C. (2001), *The ICSID Convention: A Commentary* (Cambridge University Press).

62 De Palma, A. (11 March 2001), 'North American Free Trade Agreement's Dirty Little Secret', *New York Times* 1(3).

63 Peterson, L. (2 July 2004), 'Canadian Province Rejects Public Auto Insurance; Think Tank Sees Treaty Chill', *Investment Law and Policy Weekly News Bulletin*.

Investment agreements concern the right to development. They represent the binding legal framework for the transfer of capital between developed and underdeveloped states. The right to development puts forward a contrasting structure based on global solidarity and rights-based development. It recognizes that the human rights violations resulting from globalization are failures of governance. Human rights law is capable of monitoring and regulating foreign investment. Respect for human rights requires governments to protect, promote and fulfill obligations. The right to development process can provide a framework focused on the implementation of a rights-based approach to development. The right to development is versatile and promotes global responsibility for globalization.

The Declaration on the Right to Development requires states to guarantee rights in a manner applicable to globalization. While the Declaration remains non-binding, it is a focal point of United Nations human rights activity concerning development and has been reaffirmed as a universal human right by the international community.[64] In order to be universal and remain relevant, human rights law must protect those marginalized by the exigencies of globalization by empowering local peoples.[65] It must form a bottom line below which no one can fall no matter what the economic justification may be. Human rights should be guided by the entitlements of those alienated by the globalization process rather than the property rights of those benefiting from it.[66] The United Nations General Assembly recognizes the right to development as an integral component of a just globalization process.[67]

Globalization disconnects the right to development process. Underdeveloped states are unwilling or unable to implement human rights. States have collective duties to cooperate in order to overcome this and afford developing states the opportunity to enact rights-based development policy. This responsibility should be the basis of global governance. The legal origins of this responsibility can be traced to the Charter of the United Nations[68] and its codification in the Universal Declaration of Human Rights and the International Covenant on Economic Social and Cultural Rights.[69] The Declaration on the Right to Development provides a relevant framework for applying global responsibility to global governance and development. Recognizing the economic handicap of developing states, the right to development extends entitlements and responsibility beyond national borders. The international community is responsible. This requires political will on the part of both developing and developed states, acting individually and collectively, in order to create a system in which human rights can be realized. The prioritization of foreign

---

64   Human Rights Council (15 March 2006), UNGA Res. 60/251, UN Doc. A/RES/60/251, Preamble, para.4.

65   De Feyter, K., *supra* n. 48, 3.

66   *Ibid.*

67   UNGA, 'Globalization and its impact on the full enjoyment of all human rights' (16 Dec 2005), UN Doc. A/RES/60/152, para.6 and 10.

68   The Charter of the United Nations (adopted 26 June 1945, entered into force 24 Oct 1945), 59 Stat. 1031, T.S. 993, 3 Bevans 1153.

69   International Covenant on Economic, Social and Cultural Rights (adopted 16 Dec 1996, entered into force 3 Jan 1976), G.A. Res. 2200A (XXI), 21 UN GAOR Supp. No. 16 at 49, UN Doc. A/6316 (1966), 993 U.N.T.S. 3 (ICESCR).

investment reflects a different set of national interests.[70] Existing human rights law needs to be implemented, not changed, in response to parochial self-interest.

Human rights law governs the conduct of states towards its citizens.[71] Non-state actors can violate and directly affect the provision of human rights.[72] This legal conundrum has focused attention on non-state actors.[73] Is the state-centric human rights law system relevant to the problems of economic globalization? Can non-state actors be regulated in order to play a beneficial role in the right to development process when their interests are secured through investment laws? The decline of state sovereignty over domestic policy has created a regulatory vacuum that is being filled by non-participatory and unaccountable entities.[74]

Thus, the right to development faces challenges in a globalized world. Human rights law developed at a time when international relations were the domain of states alone. Accordingly, the system of human rights protection mirrored this state-centric structure.[75] In simpler times, a centrally organized system for governing security, economic and social development was envisioned. States had responsibility towards their own inhabitants. Individuals held rights connecting to their own state. There was little recognized scope for the interference with human rights by non-state actors and the international community. The state was the only actor considered to have the capacity to violate and protect these rights at the national level.[76] Economic globalization has altered these basic premises of the human rights regime. In many cases, direct responsibility for the fulfillment of entitlements is disjointed. Accountability is further altered by the international structure of the corporate sector, which operates globally in various national legal systems.[77]

As a response, many within the human rights community now call for the direct regulation of corporations under human rights law.[78] Some advocates consider the

---

70   De Feyter, K., *supra* n. 48, 20.

71   Humphrey, J. (1991), 'The International Law of Human Rights in the Middle of the Twentieth Century', in Lillich, R., *International Human Rights: Problems of Law, Policy and Practice* (2nd edn, Boston: Little, Brown and Co.), 1.

72   See generally, Report of the Secretary-General (2 July 1996), 'The Realization of Economic, Social and Cultural Rights: The Impact of the Activities and Working Methods of Transnational Corporations on the Full Enjoyment of All Human Rights, in Particular Economic, Social and Cultural Rights and the Right to Development, Bearing in Mind Existing International Guidelines, Rules and Standards Relating to the Subject-Matter' UN Doc. E/CN.4/Sub.2/1996/12; Orentlicher, D. and Gelatt, T. (1993), 'Public Law, Private Actors: The Impact of Human Rights on Business Investors in China', *North Western Journal of International Law and Business* 14, 66.

73   Clapham, A. (2006), *Human Rights Obligations of Non-State Actors* (Oxford University Press), 2.

74   Thomas, C. (1998), 'International Financial Institutions and Social and Economic Rights: An Exploration', in Evans, T. (ed.), *Human Rights Fifty Years On: A Reappraisal* (Manchester University Press), 182.

75   Shaw, M., *supra* n. 55, 250-54.

76   *Ibid.*

77   Stephens, B., *supra* n. 24, 39.

78   Clapham, A., *supra* n. 73, 6.

state-centric system exclusionary and increasingly irrelevant.[79] Corporations are able to avoid stringent national regulations or persuade against the adoption of rights-based regulation.[80] They are also able to outsource their illegitimate activities or criminal behavior to subsidiaries in states with less stringent regulations.[81] National regulatory systems are unable to keep up with the speed of this change. States, instead of adapting and promoting regulation matching the merging global paradigm, acquiesce and allow for the further erosion of the regulatory role to further a perceived competitiveness in the race for investment. Global civil society demands universal respect for human rights despite these challenges.[82] New ways of understanding global human rights law may be needed that take into account a more diverse set of actors and responsibilities.[83]

Corporations have duties and obligations under international human rights law. They have begun to accept increased responsibility in conjunction with their increased role in international relations and human rights development. Voluntary initiatives created by the private sector, independently and in partnership with various levels of civil society have started to fill the regulatory gap. Corporate social responsibility is a welcomed venture that indicates a willingness of corporations to be part of the answer to the globalization and human rights law dilemma.

The problem remains with accountability. As a general rule, the home-state of the corporation takes the view that it is not concerned with human rights violations committed in another state by one of its corporations. And yet at the same time, states act to protect their corporations through investment treaties. That is to say, they are intensely concerned about what 'their' corporations do abroad, but they do not seem to be concerned about the human rights violations in which these corporations are involved or the negative affect their interests may have on rights-based development. The home-states continually resist the regulation of corporations internationally, fearing lost profits and competitiveness. Likewise, voluntary corporate social responsibility is unlikely to address these issues satisfactorily as it turns attention to the corporation itself, rather than to the state.

It is the state that has proven largely ineffective at regulation despite calls from civil society to ensure human rights fulfillment. States are unwilling to prioritize human rights law and appear to be highly influenced by organized lobbying from corporations. The rights of the people are then subject to the whims of whoever controls the political process. State regulation of corporations is tenuous where:

> ... the leaderships are dependent on these same foreign interests for their social and political survival. It should be recognized that foreign investors are inherently part and parcel of the political economies within which they operate. To say that they should not 'intervene'

79   *Ibid.*, 7.
80   Blumberg, P. (1993), *The Multinational Challenge to Corporation Law: The Search for a New Corporate Personality* (5th edn, Cambridge University Press), 205.
81   Garoupa, N. (2004), 'The Economics of Business Crime', in Sjogren, H. and Skogh, G. (eds), *New Perspectives on Economic Crime* (Cheltenham, UK: Edward Elgar), 12.
82   Clapham, A., *supra* n. 73, 7.
83   Teubner, G. (1997), '"Global Bukowina": Legal Pluralism in World Society', in Teubner, G. (ed.), *Global Law Without a State* (London: Dartsmouth), 5.

in the internal affairs of the countries they operate in is absurd and demonstrates the nature of legal thinking that fails to recognize the integrated nature of foreign capital. Provisions on the duty of states to regulate the activities of transnational corporations are also only relevant if one assumes a political leadership whose social interests and ideology stands in contradiction to those of such foreign institutions. [84]

Therefore a triadic system, undertaken at the micro, macro and meso-levels of regulation, must be developed. The micro-level is an economic term referring to the domain of action and decision-making taken at the individual level. In this case, it refers to the activities of individual people and corporations. The macro-level of regulation is the rules system in which the activity of corporations is undertaken. This is primarily regulated at the national level by States, which make up the second set of actors in this triad. The state must take into account the views and interests of all stakeholders within its borders, including local minority and indigenous groups. The meso-level refers to the concrete and instructional or abstract and discursive coordination systems regulated by the international community.[85] Here, the obligations of states to cooperate internationally in ensuring the functionality of the micro and macro-levels are paramount. In addition, the activities of international organizations such as financial institutions and non-governmental organizations should also be considered and monitored in accordance with the right to development. This third component must create a foundation upon which the first two components can rest. The emerging cooperative system of global governance must form the third level of responsibility. Without international cooperation, developing states are unable to hold corporations liable or protect their domestic policy-making ability at the macro level. Likewise, in the absence of international cooperation and monitoring, corporate social responsibility can be reduced to a public relations exercise. The meso-level is the most underdeveloped, but a gap between the general rules on specific action is apparent throughout.

The reason for this triadic approach to regulating corporations is that it gleans the practicable elements of the corporate social responsibility agenda and the direct human rights responsibility of corporations, the human rights obligations of both home and host-states, as well as the duties of the international community to cooperate for the realization of human rights and social development. It is hoped that avoiding the persistent discussion over which actor is directly responsible, this comprehensive approach will actually begin to deal with the failure of the international community as a whole to ensure the right to development. Rights-based development in a global world influenced by corporations as well as the home and host-states requires this triadic approach to governance. Clearly, the micro, macro and meso-levels of governance are interdependent. Addressing one level of the triad, while ignoring another, renders the entire system ineffectual.

---

84 Gutto, S. (1984), 'Responsibility and Accountability of States, Transnational Corporations and Individuals in the Field of Human Rights to Social Development: A Critique', *Third World Legal Studies Association, Human Rights and Development*, 180-81.

85 These terms are borrowed from Wayne Sandholtz and Alec Stone Sweet, see Sandholtz, W. and Stone Sweet, A. (2004), 'Law, Politics and International Governance', in Reus-Smit, C. (ed.), *The Politics of International Law* (Cambridge University Press), 239.

The world is now more poly-centric than the post-war climate human rights law was designed to regulate. Nevertheless, pressure on states for the implementation of human rights law must be maintained. States are the most accountable to governance in international relations. The monitoring and enforcement of human rights law remains nationally based and subject to national interests. Shifting human rights responsibility away from states may play into the hands of recalcitrant states, and allow them to avoid responsibility. The problem with extending exclusive human rights responsibility beyond the state is evident. Human rights law has not overcome national interests in a system consisting of less than two hundred states. How can human rights law responsibility be extended to hundreds of thousands of non-state actors, each with their own interests, and with little or no independent accountability outside of state monitoring functions?

Despite the new challenges arising from the globalization process and non-state actors, the state remains the only full subject of international law responsible under human rights law. It is the state, acting individually or collectively, that ultimately controls international relations. It creates the framework and rules in which the relevant non-state actors thrive. Despite human rights law's predilection for liberalism, realism, which prioritizes national interests, is still the prominent paradigm of international relations.[86] National interests are still the priority of international relations and human rights law is consistently subordinated to them. It is important for the human rights community to display in clear terms why global governance based on human rights is in the interest of dominant states.

The layout of the book is as follows: Part 1 focuses on the different versions of international cooperation. Chapter 2, Human Rights and Development Cooperation in Context, anchors human rights within the context of global governance based on international investment and globalization. The chapter highlights the problems associated with a system that dislocates governmental regulatory ability and domestic populations. The chapter goes on to analyze the impact of two global projects, the first human rights and the second foreign investment. The prioritization of the latter and its persistent impediment to human rights within the development process is outlined. Chapter 1 observes that foreign investment, rather than the right to development, has become synonymous with international development. The positive and negative aspects of this development system are scrutinized. The debate is important. If economic globalization is viewed as positive, then no further regulation is required. On the other hand, if economic globalization's exigencies are considered intolerable then regulation is required. The chapter then examines the influence of corporations on the development project and its ability to undermine a state's regulatory function, emphasizing the continued role of the state. The concepts of economic justice and equality are examined as the basis of governance and are linked to human rights law, in particular, economic, social and cultural rights. The chapter concludes by linking these ideas to the investment system, and suggests that global governance must be guided by a process conducive to the realization of human rights.

---

86   Forsythe, D. (2006), *Human Rights in International Relations* (2nd edn, Cambridge University Press), 251.

Chapter 3, entitled Development Cooperation in Theory: The Right to Development, focuses on the commitments of the international community to a rights-based process of development. It presents the right to development as the best indication of rights-based global governance. The Declaration on the Right to Development is an informative interpretation of states' commitments to international cooperation. The chapter outlines the content of the right to development and its legal basis. It highlights the importance of the right to development and its evolution into its present form. Fundamentally, Chapter 3 outlines the duties arising from the right to development, its legal basis and its subjects and duty bearers. It is here that the right to development is shown to be applicable to global governance thanks to its approach based on international solidarity with rights and responsibilities that transcend national borders. The right to development is conditional. It is restricted to those states implementing a rights-based process of development nationally and can only be used in conjunction with a participatory and accountable system. For clarification, the framework of the rights based process is outlined. This limitation is essential in preventing elite capture. While the Declaration does not impose binding legal responsibilities, it is a source of law. It should create important norms for national and international economic and political policy-making. It provides a basis to hold governments accountable to their own populations for their international actions.

Chapter 4, Development Cooperation in Practice: International Investment Law outlines contemporary international cooperation for development. It details the barriers to human rights presented by the collective action of states through the network of bilateral investment treaties. This chapter explains the emergence of binding standards on the treatment of foreign investors that conflict with the right to development. It examines the unsure evolution of these standards and their potential reduction of the state's regulatory ability through the prioritization of developed state's national interests. Chapter 4 looks at various ways that human rights discourse might be included in investment law. It examines how the emerging norms of investment are confronting human rights law in a number of pending cases. These include cases involving equality in South Africa, public services in Argentina and indigenous rights in a number of other states. Direct challenges to governmental public purpose regulations can result in an institutionalized reduction the regulatory ability of states. It remains to be seen whether human rights law will be prioritized in the investment arbitration process.[87]

Part 2 searches for a framework for international cooperation and suggests a tripartite system of micro, macro and meso-level responsibility. This means that corporations, states and the international community must abide by legal, political/ economic and moral obligations to ensure that developing states retain policy-making space to implement the right to development. The regulation of influential non-state actors is addressed in light of a paradigm shift in international relations.

Chapter 5 looks at the micro-level of regulation. It examines the important advances made by the corporate social responsibility movement. Chapter 5 looks in

---

87 *Methanex Corporation v. United States of America*, in the Matter of an Arbitration under Chapter 11 of the North American Free Trade Agreement and the UNCITRAL Arbitration Rules, Final Award of the Tribunal on Jurisdiction and Merits, 3 Aug 2005.

depth at the direct legal responsibility of corporations under human rights law and examines the Draft Norms on the Responsibility of Transnational Corporations.[88] These advances are discussed and criticized in relation to problems at all three levels of the tripartite system proposed in Part 2.

The macro-level of regulation is developed in Chapter 6. As the primary decision makers in international relations states should retain the primary duty for fulfilling human rights law. In doing so, they must hold corporations liable for direct violations and retain their regulatory function despite corporate pressures. This chapter addresses the framework of international law regarding the horizontal application of human rights law and the responsibility to protect of host-states. It provides a detailed examination of the increasingly important role of the home-state and the potential for extraterritorial application of home-state human rights laws.

The meso-level is the essential component of regulation examined in Chapter 7. Global governance should be based on international human rights law obligations. The framework for international law applicable to international cooperation is traced. The chapter draws upon the international legal obligations of states to international cooperation. It emphasizes political commitments to collective security that prioritizes cooperation for human development. It deals with realist international relations and human rights. Development and human rights are put in terms of national security and national interest to further engrain the need to promote the right to development.

The concluding chapter looks at the value added of the right to development as a framework for global governance. The right to development could be used as a tool for evaluating global development policy, including investment treaties. The concluding chapter examines the problems of realism and national sovereignty and briefly discusses ways in which international cooperation can overcome such barriers. Rights-based development is emphasized citing the linkage between human development and political stability. Stability is the foundation for investment, economic growth and global security. The business case for the right to development is put forward with similar goals. The purpose of this is to convince states that rights-based development, including the regulation of non-state actors, is in their own best national security and economic interests. The concluding chapter also contains a commentary on the international cooperation, interdependence and the changing nature of sovereignty. The book concludes with a last word promoting international cooperation for human rights law in order to improve and legitimize economic globalization. A final warning is issued based on historical lessons of past attempts at economic globalization. When profit creation outstrips the ability of societies to protect and promote their own social, economic and cultural goals, a backlash against the economic system is inevitable. Emerging responses to contemporary economic globalization are noted.

88　Draft Norms on the Responsibilities of Transnational Corporations and Other Business Enterprises with Regard to Human Rights (2003) E/CN.4/Sub.2/2003/12.

PART 1
Development in a Global World

Chapter 2

Human Rights and Development Cooperation in Context

Introduction

Human rights in development face a conundrum; foreign investment and corporations are required for economic growth, yet they can undermine the provision of rights. De Schutter comments on the necessary evil of investment stating that, 'For all the ill feelings that the acts of certain transnational corporations have aroused in developing countries where they have operated, there is one thing that is worse than to attract foreign direct investment: it is to attract none.'[1] The international community has forged a market-based system of development, where investment is allocated according to the potential to profit. Investment is allocated unevenly with large swathes of the developing world, much of which in dire need of development, being left out of globalization. Gilpin explains that, ' ... the least developed countries in Africa and elsewhere have received a pitifully small percentage of the total amount invested in the developing world. Need it be said that these skewed statistics do not fit the image of globalization!'[2]

The absence of an organized global development strategy based on more than economic growth necessitates foreign investment. The challenge is for states to gain or retain the ability to utilize foreign investment to promote sustainable and rights-based development without fear of corporate divestment.

Economic globalization has been wildly successful in terms of expanding investment and trade. However, since the late 1990s, problems concerning human rights and the environment have emerged that threaten to undermine the legitimacy and achievements of economic globalization.[3] More and more developing states are veering off the path of economic globalization, adopting nationalist and protectionist measures in order to retain wealth for development purposes.

Globalization, from a western perspective, involves the widening, deepening and speeding up of worldwide inter-connected economic and social life, from the

---

1 De Schutter, O. (2005), 'Transnational Corporations as Instruments of Human Development', in Alston, P. and Robinson, M. (eds), *Human Rights and Development: Towards Mutual Reinforcement* (Oxford University Press), 403.

2 Gilpin, R. (2000), *The Challenge of Global Capitalism: The World Economy in the 21st Century* (Princeton University Press), 170.

3 While recognizing the interdependence and relevance of environmental and sustainable development issues, the discourse here is limited to human rights and the right to development.

cultural to the criminal, to the financial and the spiritual.[4] This process has been deemed inevitable and granted an almost natural status above any other system of economic and political organization. Alston explains that:

> ... the means which are always assumed to be an indispensable part of the globalization process, have in fact acquired the status of values in and of themselves. Those means/ values include, for example: privatization of as many functions as possible; deregulation, particularly of private power, at both the national and international levels; reliance upon the free market as the most efficient and appropriate value-allocating mechanism; minimal international regulation except in relation to 'new' international agenda items.[5]

The developed world insists, 'there is no alternative' to neoliberal economic globalization.[6] It follows that states are unable to avoid joining agreements that promote liberalization.[7] In 1998, Tony Blair insisted that there is no choice except liberalization. In a similar vein, Bill Clinton explained that, 'globalization is not a policy choice'.[8] The developing world perceives economic globalization as Western dominance. Shiva argues that there is a contradiction between a natural process and one that the G-7 continually promotes: 'It may seem puzzling why these oracles of the globe go to such great lengths to bring about something that exists already or is inexorable.'[9]

Globalization has had influence on the international relations, altering the way states interact. Economic globalization presents a challenge to the human rights law designed for the previous model of international relations. Yet the problems associated with economic globalization and human rights are not unavoidable. Alternatives remain possible. Despite the precedence afforded globalization, the significance of its penetration may be misunderstood.[10] Goodin offers this informal and novel experiment:

> Go to your closet. Look at the labels of your shirts. If globalization is true, why don't all the labels say 'made in China'? (Indeed, why do none of them say 'Burkina Faso', where unit labour costs are even lower?) Go to the Kitchen. Up-end your favourite half dozen

4   Held, D. et al. (1999), *Global Transformation: Politics, Economics and Culture* (Cambridge: Polity Press), 2.

5   Alston, P. (1997), 'The Myopia of the Handmaidens: International Lawyers and Globalization', *European Journal of International Law* 8, 442.

6   Margaret Thatcher coined the phrase 'There Is No Alternative' now referred to as TINA. Boucher, D. (1999), *The Paradox of Plenty: Hunger in a Bountiful World* (California: Food First), 274.

7   Ralston Saul, J. (1995), *The Collapse of Globalism and the Reinvention of the World* (Penguin), 12.

8   Shiva, V. (1999), 'Food Rights, Free Trade and Fascism', in Gibney, M. (ed.), *Globalizing Rights* (Oxford University Press), 88.

9   Fitzpatrick, R., 'Globalism' (paper presented at the conference on the future of human rights, Warwick University, 14 Dec 1998), quoted in Shiva, V. *Ibid.* 89.

10   See Cable, V. (1995), 'The Diminished Nation-State: A Study in the Loss of Economic Power', *Daedalus* 124.2, 24.

appliances. If globalization is true, why do any of them say 'Made in Germany' where unit labour costs are so high?[11]

Economic globalization is not unilaterally reshaping the global economy. It is not beyond the control of states. Indeed, foreign investment seems attracted to some of the most regulated states such as the United States, Germany, Japan, China and Canada. Although alternatives are labeled self-destructive and inefficient,[12] individual states retain a policy-making ability that attracts investment.[13] This is reflected in the state-centric structure of international law.

The formulation of international law, its implementation and its relevance, is determined through international relations and national policies.[14] The implementation of human rights law is primarily accomplished through domestic law frameworks.[15] States retain the ability to govern national policies and domestic economies. They are therefore the principal determinants of economic affairs affecting human rights.[16] International law gives domestic populations sovereignty over their territory; the state governs on their behalf. Accordingly, states are free to decide their own policy in conformance with the norms of the international community.[17] This includes economic policy such as standard setting for the admission and regulation of foreign investment.[18]

The term 'host-state' refers to the state that the corporation invests in. The 'home-state' houses the corporation's headquarters. Home and host-state relations are complicated by foreign investment. In theory, investment in a host-state is mutually beneficial, generating profits for corporations in return for tax revenue, technology transfer and economic growth for the host. Yet, conflicts have arisen in this relationship. For example, a host-state can expropriate or nationalize the property of the home-state's corporation. These situations have resulted in inter-state conflict

---

11 Gooden, R. (2003), 'Globalizing Justice', in Held, D. and Koenig-Archibugi, M. (eds), *Taming Globalization: Frontiers of Governance* (Cambridge: Polity Press), 69.

12 See, Pfaller, A., Gough, I. and Therborn, G. (1991), *Can the Welfare State Compete? A Comparative Study of Five Advanced Capitalist Economies* (London: Macmillan); Held D. et al., *supra* n.4.

13 Gooden, R., *supra* n.11, 69.

14 Forsythe, D. (2006), *Human Rights in International Relations* (2nd edn, Cambridge University Press), 252.

15 Clapham, A. (2005), *Human Rights Obligations of Non-State Actors* (Oxford University Press), 437.

16 Gilpin, R. (2001), *Global Political Economy: Understanding the International Economic Order* (Princeton University Press), 3.

17 Evans, M. (2003), *International Law* (5th edn, Cambridge University Press), 254 and 411.

18 United Nations Conference on Trade and Development (1999), *Series on International Investment Agreements: Admission and Establishment*, UNCTAD/ITE/IIT/10 (vol. II), 8.

in the past.[19] Diplomatic and economic relations can be harmed by the treatment of foreign investment by hosts and the reaction by home-states.[20]

The doctrine of state sovereignty assumes that host-states can regulate activities in their own territories. Liberalization and deregulation have as their main objective the reduction of the role of the state.[21] This process leaves sectors previously controlled by states in the hands of non-state actors.[22] Concerns surrounding the distribution of wealth created by foreign investment activities are now raised. Regulation of investment is crucial to the host-state's ability to benefit from this situation.[23] While corporations have not replaced the state, their activities hold considerable sway over policy-making.[24] This is not new, but is increasingly visible as investors' influence grows. A relationship of dependency, both to foreign investors and developed states for political, economic and security reasons, influences policy decisions.[25]

The role of the state in an era of economic globalization is crucial to human rights in development. State power has been conceded in the economic arena, with immediate consequences for human rights. The provision of human rights can no longer be limited to individual states. The international community must empower institutions that enable individual states to deal with pressures arising from globalization. Nevertheless, the international community seems reluctant to do so.[26]

The loss of the regulatory function by host-states is often pointed to as evidence of the decline of the nation-state. Yet, the current period of 'fragmentation'[27] is characterized by the failure to implement a cosmopolitan framework to replace states.[28] Instead neoliberal economic principles have achieved hegemony. Liberalism emphasizes free markets and individualism. Both political liberals and conservatives now promote liberal economics. Neoliberalism is based on a return to *laissez-faire*

---

19   See generally, Rodman, K. (1988), *Sanctity versus Sovereignty: US Policy Towards the Nationalization of Natural Resource Investments in the Third World* (Columbia University Press).

20   See 'Exxon Cut off from Venezualan Oil'. *CNN.com/World* (published online 21 Feb 2008 <http://edition.cnn.com/2008/WORLD/americas/02/12/venezuela.oil.ap/index.html?eref=rss_world>, accessed 10 March 2008).

21   Ralston Saul, J., *supra* n.7, 74-5.

22   *Ibid.*; see also De Feyter K. and Gomez, I. (eds) (2005), *Privatisation and Human Rights in the Age of Globalization* (Antwerp: Intersentia).

23   Aside from investment disputes, conflict can arise from protectionist trade policies and monetary policy. However, these important aspects of economic globalization are beyond the scope of this book.

24   Addo, M. (ed.) (1999), *Human Rights Standards and the Responsibility of Transnational Corporations* (The Hague: Kluwer Law International), 4.

25   Goldstein, J. (2003), *International Relations* (5th edn, New York: Longman), 367.

26   See Skogly, S. (2001), *The Human Rights Obligations of the World Bank and the International Monetary Fund* (London: Cavendish).

27   Rosenau, J. (1997), *Along the Domestic-Foreign Frontier: Exploring Governance in a Turbulent World* (Cambridge University Press), 38.

28   Held, D. (2006), 'Reframing Global Governance: Apocalypse Soon or Reform?' (Annual Political Science Lecture, Carleton University, 19 Oct 2006).

liberalism requiring the reduction of state regulations.[29] It requires the prioritization of economic growth, liberalization of trade and investment, consumerism, and the promotion of corporations in development.[30]

Human rights are threatened by neoliberal economic globalization as they depend on the sovereign power of the state for implementation and enforcement. The United Nation's human rights system revolves around holding states accountable. The state has been shown to be reluctant to regulate in the face of economic globalization. Unregulated economic globalization has led to rising poverty, homelessness, landlessness, violence and environmental destruction.[31] In 2003 the poorest 20 per cent of the world had 1 per cent of global income, down from 1.4 per cent in 1991 and 2.3 per cent in 1960. The ratio between the top 20 per cent and the bottom 20 per cent in global income terms has risen from 30 to 1 in 1960 to 78 to 1 by 1994.[32]

The World Bank claims that the average level of real income in the richest countries is 50 times that of the poorest.[33] This level of social and economic inequality results in differences in access to political power, to justice, and to food, shelter, healthy environments and health care. This undermines the legitimacy of democratic institutions. External actors, such as corporations and international organizations, are then perceived as more powerful and influential.[34] Inequality is linked to poverty. Combating income inequality is the key to economic, social and cultural rights, and requires regulation.

Neoliberal principles directly threaten these human rights. Favourable conditions of work are undermined by an emphasis on competitiveness. Social security is privatized. Health care and education funding is cut in order to meet monetary policy demands. The Committee on Economic, Social and Cultural Rights has identified these problems and has called for a renewed commitment to respect economic, social and cultural rights.[35] This presents a fundamental challenge that individual states cannot face alone. Action to promote human rights at the national level increasingly requires international cooperation in a globalized world. The right to development has corresponding international obligations calling for a collective role of states.

There are positive examples of state regulation working towards human rights development. By committing significant portions of gross domestic product to

---

29   Felice, W. (2003), *The Global New Deal: Economic and Social Human Rights in World Politics* (Lanham, Md.: Rowman and Littlefield), 30.

30   *Ibid.*

31   *Ibid.*

32   United Nations Development Programme (1997), *Human Development Report, 1997* (Oxford University Press), 9.

33   World Bank (2004), *World Development Report 2004: Making Services Work for Poor People* (Oxford University Press).

34   Luis Arbour, 'Lafontaine-Baldwin Symposium Speech 2005' (Quebec City, March 2005), (available online <www.lafontaine-baldwin.com/speeches/2005/>, accessed 10 March 2008).

35   Committee on Economic, Social and Cultural Rights, 'Statement on globalization and economic, social and cultural rights: May 1998', para.4 (available online at: <www. unhchr.ch/tbs/doc.nsf/0/0fad637e6f7a89d580256738003eef9a?OpenDocument>, accessed 10 March 2008).

education, health care and basic infrastructure, developing states such as Sri Lanka, Kerala (India), Botswana, and Costa Rica for example, have realized social development despite varying levels of economic growth.[36] These states have ignored neoliberal trends. Instead they have developed state-supported public services, invested in health and education before economic take-off, and in health education and affirmative action for women.[37] This model has resulted in sustained growth.

The ability to regulate is restricted through bilateral negotiations between the host and home-states. Investment treaties facilitate the operations of corporations. While the corporation has the leverage to take its investment elsewhere, once established, their investment is long term.[38] The home-state brings all of its political and economic influence to the table, ensuring favourable conditions and protection for its own economic interests.[39] The corporations then carry out these interests privately.[40] Many states are complicit in reducing their own ability to regulate by granting unaccountable privileges to corporations. The fact that foreign investment protection requires international agreements undermines the argument that economic globalization has overtaken the state. The state is still required to facilitate and protect the corporation and it does so willingly through legally binding treaties.[41]

Two Global Projects

The two global projects examined are investment and human rights. The term 'project' is used here to denote the process of state action in formulating and implementing norms through international cooperation. Non-state actors also influence these projects. The investment project is based on corporate interests while the human rights project is influenced by civil society through the actions of non-governmental organizations. Both projects are similar. They have global reach and transcend national legal systems. They both affect the development of international law and make inroads into domestic sovereignty.

The investment project is characterized by aggrandizement of the power of corporations, the influence of capital markets, and the expansion of investment as a catalyst for economic development. Corporate interests are the most important in bilateral treaties between states. The human rights project is characterized by a spread of a universal and interdependent code of legally binding rights for human beings.[42] The result has been the emergence of an international system supported by regional human rights regimes in Europe, the Americas and Africa, burgeoning

---

36   Felice, W., *supra* n.29, 32-6.
37   Mehrotra, S. (1997), 'Social Development in High Achieving Countries: Common Elements and Diversities', in Mehrotra S. and Jolly R. (eds), *Development with a Human Face* (Clarendon Press), 29.
38   Gilpin, R., *supra* n.16, 297.
39   Goldstein, J., *supra* n.25, 367.
40   Gilpin, R., *supra* n.16, 297.
41   Goldstein, J., *supra* n.25, 367.
42   See Kinley, D. (2005), 'Human Rights, the Rule of Law and Globalization: Friends, Foes or Family?', *UCLA Journal of International Law and Foreign Affairs* 7, 245.

rudimentary developments in the Arab states, with a notable gap in Asia.[43] However, the implementation and adherence to the human rights framework cannot be compared to that of the investment project, which is binding on states.

Economic globalization in practice contradicts the notion of an orderly procession towards a global legal order. The lack of a centralized law-making authority for development results in a fragmented process based on developed world national economic interests.[44] The investment project has forged ahead unregulated in terms of human rights. Meanwhile, the implementation of human rights law in development cooperation is delayed as it may reduce the profitability of the investment project. This failure creates a sociological sense of inevitability concerning entrenched inequalities.[45] It shrouds the contemporary international hierarchy in impunity and renders alternatives for responsibility unacceptable.

While the projects of international investment and international human rights development appear to be incongruent, there are convergences between the two. Human rights and investment are not mutually exclusive. Human rights enjoyment can secure a stable political climate for investment while foreign investment can result in economic growth. If managed properly, this can result in increased resources available for human rights fulfillment.[46] Human rights advocates criticize the process of economic globalization for its distributional inequality. International cooperation on redistribution would allow for human rights standards to assume a more prominent position economic globalization. The right to development focuses squarely on this problem.

Both global projects have international and national dimensions.[47] The investment project has penetrated state sovereignty more effectively than human rights law. Not many states violate the investment agenda of deregulation, structural adjustment, and market liberalization. Even if opposed by domestic populations, foreign investors have been granted extensive protection for market exploitation. The effectiveness of both projects rests upon their domestic implementation. States have conflicting legal obligations under human rights and foreign investment treaties.[48]

The legal aspects of these movements are only part of the overall ideology, which in one case is the promotion of human dignity, and the other, property rights. Neither can rely solely on courts and tribunals.[49] Broad political and economic considerations must be factored into both equations. Both projects require domestic political support, in which education plays an important role. Human rights are more

---

43   *Ibid.*

44   Teubner, G. (1997), '"Global Bukowina": Legal Pluralism in the World Society', in Teubner G. (ed.), *Global Law Without a State* (Aldershot: Dartmouth), 5-6.

45   Jochnick, C. (1999), 'Confronting the Impunity of Non-State Actors: New Fields for the Promotion of Human Rights', *Human Rights Quarterly* 21.1, 58.

46   Kinley, D. (2002), 'Human Rights, the Rule of Law and Globalization: Friends, Foes or Family?', *UCLA Journal of International Law and Foreign Affairs* 7, 245.

47   *Ibid.* p.242

48   0Marceau, G. (2002), 'WTO Dispute Settlement and Human Rights', *European Journal of International Law* 13.4, 60.

49   See Kinley, D. (1998), 'The Legal Dimension of Human Rights', *Human Rights in Australian Law* 2.

precarious. If people are not aware of the nature of their needs as entitlements and governments do not view their obligations as legal duties towards their populations there can be no effective human rights realization.

Human rights law defends the rights of the marginalized and promotes stability. Although violations persist, the law provides a sound basis for criticism of economic globalization. Law subjects human conduct to rules; it does not prevent unlawful behavior.[50] To judge international human rights law by its failure to prevent human rights violations is unsound. Murder is illegal in national law but that does not prevent its occurrence. The goal of the human rights project is to establish a framework of law governing state action towards citizens. This system comprises rules of general application. States are bound by rules; and these rules should be publicly accessible so that the legal implications of state policy can be challenged.[51]

The same technical forces of change that facilitate global investment also facilitate the expansion of human rights norms. Advancements in technology and communications have enhanced the ability of civil society, NGOs and activists to operate beyond national borders.[52] It has ensured that control of information is difficult, thereby allowing ideas to circulate world wide, promoting the growth of universal values and human rights.

Are these two legal frameworks – one regulating investment and one regulating human rights – contradictory or can their apparently irreconcilable agendas converge? This is the pressing issue for development and human rights. Global civil society has disclosed that the investment project, despite being profitable, has not necessarily ensured human rights for the disadvantaged.[53] Global trends should not be the focus of the human rights activists; rather, it is their use and content as formulated by states that should be considered. Both frameworks rely upon political will for their implementation despite changes brought on by economic globalization. In a globalized world, it is obvious where the political will to compromise sovereignty lies.

States and the Prioritization of Investment

Economic globalization did not evolve or occur naturally. Its social costs cannot be blamed entirely on the powerful non-state actors it promotes. Neoliberal economists insist that an international economy based on free trade automatically emerges if governments do not interfere. However, this non-interference requires drastic policy changes in many circumstances. It is risky politically for a state to remove itself from regulatory duties. This action can result in many resentful losers and produce only a few, albeit influential, winners.

---

50   *Ibid.*

51   Kinley, D., *supra* n.46, 247.

52   Streeten, P. (1999), 'Globalization and its Impact on Development Co-operation', *Development* 42.3, 11.

53   Shelton, D. (2002), 'Symposium: Globalization and the Erosion of Sovereignty in Honour of Prof. Litchenstein: Protecting Human Rights in a Globalised World', *Boston College International and Comparative Law Revue* 25, 278.

The United States of America has made a concerted effort since World War II to create economic globalization outside of its borders. This effort included the promotion of the Reciprocal Trade Act of 1934, the Bretton Woods Agreements of 1944, and regional strengthening during the Cold War.[54] The strategy included the Marshall Plan for Europe. The plan ensured Western Europe did not succumb to the Soviet threat and joined its economy in an open relationship with the United States. The use of political and economic power created an open economy that defined the relationships between most states.[55] The role of a dominant state is apparent in the organization and creation of an international economic system.

Economic globalization also has foundations in the neoliberal world order put forward in the 1980s through Reaganomics and Thatcherism.[56] States have consciously made decisions, both collectively and individually, that have exacerbated the problems of globalization.[57] These choices included economic liberalization, deregulation and privatization. States formed international financial institutions that advocated the Washington Consensus.[58] Globalization is a result of conscious decisions made by powerful states for economic, political and security reasons.[59]

While states remain the most important actors, there is no doubt that their policies are conditioned, constrained and influenced by a variety of non-state actors. There are highly influential interest groups within states, which comprise a group of sub-state actors.[60] These groups of companies, consumers, workers, investors and cultural groups are organized and politically motivated, operating through lobbying, political action committees and other means. These groups affect international politics.[61] However, not all of these groups wield equal influence. For example, indigenous peoples often have much less say in economic decision making than powerful corporate lobbyists. Sklair refers to this influential group as the transnational capitalist class and describes it as follows:

---

54   Gilpin, R., *supra* n.16, 43.

55   *Ibid.*

56   Reinisch, A. (2005), 'The Changing International Legal Framework for Dealing with Non-State Actors', in Alston P. (ed.), *Non-State Actors and Human Rights* (Oxford University Press), 77.

57   Gilpin, R., *supra* n.16, 9.

58   Higgot, R. (2001), 'Economic Globalization and Global Governance: Towards a Post Washington Consensus', in Rittberger, V. (ed.), *Global Governance and the United Nations System* (United Nations University Press), 127.

59   For the original theory of hegemonic power in the creation of economic systems see Hallet Carr, E. (1951), *The Twenty Years Crisis, 1919–1939: An Introduction to the Study of International Relations* (London: MacMillan). Edward Hallet Carr connects the failure of international economic cooperation in this era with the decline of the hegemonic power, in this case Britain, required to govern such a system.

60   Goldstein, J., *supra* n.25, 12.

61   Milner, H. (1997), *Interests, Institutions and Information: Domestic Politics and International Relations* (Princeton Universtiy Press); Snyder, J. (1991), *Myths of Empire: Domestic Politics and International Ambition* (London: Cornell Studies in Security Affairs Series).

The TCC [transnational capitalist class] consists of people who see their own interests and/or the interests of their social and/or ethnic group, often transformed into an imagined national interest, as best served by an identification with the interests of the capitalist global system. In particular, the interests of those who own and control the major transnational corporations dictated the interests of the system as a whole.[62]

This group is the driving force of domestic economies that have increasingly international effects. Thus, what were once sub-state actors now operate in a transnational manner. Dominant states attempt to influence the design and functioning of global systems in order to advance their own national interests, which reflect those of the influential lobby groups.[63] The expansion of the transnational capitalist class is bound to the efforts of states extolling their interests.[64]

Investment refers to the exchange of money for capital that will produce income for the investor, compensating them for the initial expenditure.[65] Foreign investment refers to the ownership of capital, such as buildings, factories and property. Foreign investment is one of the most politically sensitive activities of corporations. As a result, corporations now seek to use their influence to ensure that their home-states facilitate their investment operations. The corporation influences state decision making but the state still sets out rules for market functioning.[66] The entire system relies in the long term, at least partly, on state support.[67] In the end, it is the state that puts forward corporate interests before those of its indigenous and minority groups.

International organizations created by states have ranked economic concerns above human rights law.[68] This has occurred despite the human rights commitments of states.[69] The Committee on Economic Social and Cultural Rights has warned against the current system of global governance and its dangers for human rights. It clarified that:

All of these risks can be guarded against, or compensated for, if appropriate policies are put in place. The Committee is concerned, however, that while much energy and many resources have been expended by governments on promoting the trends and policies that are associated with globalization, insufficient efforts are being made to devise new or complementary approaches which could enhance the compatibility of those trends and policies with full respect for economic, social and cultural rights. Competitiveness, efficiency and economic rationalism must not be permitted to become the primary or

---

62   Sklair, L. (2002), *Globalization: Capitalism and Its Alternatives* (3rd edn, Oxford University Press), 9.

63   Gilpin, R., *supra* n.16, 78.

64   Sklair, L., *supra* n.62, 9.

65   *Ibid.*

66   Gilpin, R., *supra* n.16, 23.

67   *Ibid.* p.98.

68   Petersmann, E. (2002), 'Time for a United Nations "Global Compact" for Integrating Human Rights into the Law of Worldwide Organizations: Lessons from European Integration', *European Journal of International Law* 13, 62.

69   Wells, C. and Elias, J. 'Catching the Conscience of the King: Corporate Players on the International Stage', in Alston P. (ed.), *supra* n.56, 171.

exclusive criteria against which governmental and inter-governmental policies are evaluated.[70]

International cooperation has been coordinated exclusively in terms of facilitating profits. Investment agreements provide an excellent example.[71] The result is an international economic order that protects the property rights of corporations. By contrast, human rights, and in particular economic, social and cultural rights, are largely unimplemented and ineffective for the majority of people. Corporations are able to exploit globalization and evade responsibility for matters that are not market-based.[72]

This pattern has accelerated since the 1980s. Socialist economies have collapsed and opened up to capitalist investment. Liberalization to attract foreign investment is put forward as the only viable option for development. Developed states have pressured developing and transitional states to reduce regulation. Muchlinski notes that, 'No longer is the control of the potentially negative impacts of TNCs [transnational corporations] the major issue; rather it is how best to reintegrate developing countries into the global economy in a manner that ensures inflows of new investment capital.'[73] International civil society has reacted and demands corporate regulation and human rights accountability.

While the proponents of liberalization and deregulation are quick to back the international regulation of competition, intellectual property, and the bribery of public officials, they decry human rights regulation as unnecessary market interference.[74] If all of these areas of economic interaction are deemed within the realm of legitmate international regulation, less ethical practices such as profiting from a system conducive to human rights denial should also be regulated. There is great enthusiasm for rules that protect and facilitate private sector activities but utter disdain for those which generate accountability, possibly hampering commercial activities.[75] States must be able to ensure corporate responsibility. Human rights should be promoted at a pace equivalent to the growth of the economy. This requires the fulfillment of human rights obligations that are presently disregarded by the international community.

---

70   Committee on Economic, Social and Cultural Rights, 'Statement on globalization and economic, social and cultural rights: May 1998', *supra* n.35, para.4.

71   Fatouros, A. (ed.) (1994), *Transnational Corporations; The International Legal Framework* (United Nations Library on Transnational Corporations, Vol. 20), 83.

72   Kamminga, M. and Zia Zarifi, S. (2000), *The Liability of Multinational Corporations Under International Law* (The Hague: Kluwer Law International), 25.

73   Muchlinski, P. (1995), *Multinational Enterprises and the Law* (Oxford: Blackwell), 596.

74   Stephens, B. (2002), 'Stefan A. Reisenfeld Symposium 2001: The Amorality of Profit: Transnational Corporations and Human Rights', *Berkeley Journal of International Law* 20, 65.

75   Baker, M. (1993), 'Private Codes of Conduct: Should the Fox Guard the Henhouse?' *University of Miami Inter-American Law Review* 24, 399.

In order to fulfill human rights related goals, host-states often must confront investment agreements.[76] For example, the host-state may find that raising taxes or imposing new regulations such as affirmative action programmes or conditionality upon investor's activities is prohibited. Nationalization, where the host-state takes control of the investment itself with or without compensation in order to pay for national development programmes or to empower local groups, is not possible. These types of activities are expressly discouraged by the states through investment agreements.

It is important to note that while the ability of corporations to demand favourable terms of investment is high before they have invested, once investment has occurred, this leverage is reduced.[77] A corporation investing in a gold mine or oil refinery in a host-state cannot move such facilities once they are operational. Nevertheless, increased regulation and nationalization occur rarely, as most host-states are dependent on the global economy. They fear alienating further investment and slowing economic growth.[78]

Globalization has reduced state accountability to people and has subsequently enhanced the role of corporations. For example, in Ecuador, where land reform was enacted by the state, investors voiced their disapproval and succeeded in hindering its reorganization.[79] This investment power reinforces global inequality both within and among states.[80] It also necessitates environmental degradation, widespread exploitation, and intensified competition between economic classes and powerful interest groups.[81] These costs may prove to outweigh the benefits of economic globalization.

State Regulation and Investment

States attempt to enact foreign investment policy that promotes their particular national interests. However, home and host-state regulatory goals are diverse. Home-states are primarily concerned with the expropriation and ensuring revenue returns from foreign subsidiaries. They also want to guarantee access for their corporations to raw materials while protecting technological and managerial know-how. Home-states have demonstrated their willingness to use political and economic power to protect the global interests of their corporations.[82] This has ensured the prominence of their regulatory priorities in investment protection agreements.[83]

---

76   Shalankany, A. (2000), 'Arbitration and the Third World: A Plea for Reassessing Bias under the Specter of Neoliberalism', *Harvard International Law Journal* 41, 419.

77   Goldstein, J., *supra* n.25, 367.

78   *Ibid.*

79   'Land Battles', *The Economist* (23-29 Sept 2006), 41.

80   Wade, R. (2003), 'The Disturbing Rise in Poverty and Inequality: Is It All a Big Lie?' in Held, D. and Koenig-Archibugi, M. (eds), *supra* n.11, 32-42.

81   Sklair, L., *supra* n.62, 48-57.

82   Muchlinski, P., *supra* n.73, 103.

83   Organization for Economic Cooperation and Development (1987), *Introduction to the OECD Codes of Liberalization*, Chapter 2.

Host-states, conversely, have generally been concerned with promoting economic development. For this they require inward capital investment, new technology and lower priced goods and services. Host-states wish to protect and promote their domestic economy, which requires placing conditions on foreign investment. For example, the host-state might require a certain percentage of inputs, such as human or national resources to be sourced locally. Aside from subjecting the foreign investor to local regulatory conditions, the host-state may enact performance requirements based on technology and skill transfer or employment levels. The host-state may wish to restrict entry in order to protect domestic industry. These regulatory priorities are difficult to impose in the current regulatory environment and depend on the relative bargaining power of host-states.[84]

Regulation of investors' operations is traditionally permitted as long as it promotes public policy concerns.[85] This is an unclear area of law and its precise meaning has been difficult to determine. The prevalence within investor-state dispute resolutions of a test based upon impact on the investor rather than on the intention of regulations appears to restrict the public policy defense.[86] Such an interpretation limits the ability and flexibility of governments to undertake policy and regulatory reform in important sectors relevant to the right to development.

The system of investment protection, given its immense importance to development and connection with human rights, is inconsistent with human rights responsibility based on state sovereignty. The ability to impose rights-based regulation on foreign investment depends on a bargaining process between the host-state and the corporation within a mutually agreed framework. Dependency theory suggests that host-states are in a permanently weaker position as a result of unequal terms of investment and trade in the international economy. Thus, the host-state is exploited through a bargaining process with a more powerful corporation from a dominant home-state.[87]

The prevalence of foreign investment and its prioritization in treaty form promotes purely market-based economies with little room for governmental regulation for human rights purposes. States must regulate less in order to attract investment. Attempts to regulate are perceived to reduce a state's competitiveness in attracting foreign investment.[88] Once established, corporations make independent decisions regarding production, research and development, and technology transfer. States, committed to the welfare of citizens, must respond to these decisions while attempting to meet social objectives. This significantly reduces public policy choices for states.[89] The basic provision of human rights is ranked beneath investment interests by the

---

84   Muchlinski, P., *supra* n.73, 104.

85   Wai, R. (2002), 'Transnational Liftoff and Juridical Touchdown: The Regulatory Function of Private International Law in an Era of Globalization', *Columbia Journal of International Law* 40, 214.

86   This determination is examined in detail in Chapter 3.

87   Muchlinski, P., *supra* n.73, 105.

88   Koenig-Archibugi, M. (2003), 'Introduction: Globalization and the Challenge of Governance', in Held, D. and Koenig-Archibugi, M. (eds), *supra* n.11, 4.

89   Stopford, J. and Strange, S. (1991), *Rival States, Rival Firms* (Cambridge University Press), 214-27.

international community. As far back as 1992 the United Nations Special Rapporteur on the realization of economic, social and cultural rights recognized in his seminal report on the subject that:

> The flurry of many states romantically to embrace the market as the ultimate solution to all of society's ills, and the corresponding rush to denationalize and leave economics, politics and social matters to the whims of the private sector, although the theme of the day, will inevitably have an impact upon the full realization of economic, social and cultural rights.[90]

The inability of states to regulate effects the protection and provision of public goods, economic equality and capabilities. The theory of market failure explains the necessity for public policy to protect these concepts. Markets may meet the needs of consumers but fail to ensure public goods. Market failure occurs due to a lack of financial incentives to ensure public goods, economic equality or capability. Without government regulation, these components of development will be threatened.[91] For example, in many developing states mobile phone coverage exists where medical facilities do not!

Human rights law is primarily concerned with equality; the right to development focuses on economic equality in particular. The term public good refers to products and necessities that all people enjoy in common, and that are universal in consumption. These public goods include international peace, health, environmental sustainability and the preservation of global commons.[92] Economic equality deals with the equal provision of public goods, including nutrition, sanitation, shelter, clothing, basic education, and healthcare.[93]

Equality may be viewed as having two components, termed formal equality and material equality. Formal or *de jure* equality means equal treatment in law, and material or *de facto* equality can be described as economic, social and cultural equality.[94] Economic equality forms the basis of economic, social and cultural rights and is emphasized in the right to development process. It is contingent on public policy enacted to ameliorate deprivations and create equality through measures promoting health care, sanitation, unemployment insurance, job retraining, public education etc.[95] In order to benefit from such measures, capabilities must be promoted. Capability depends on adequate nutrition, health, self-respect and participation. The capabilities approach measures ways in which people are permitted to achieve

90   Türk, D. (3 July 1992), 'The Realization of Economic, Social and Cultural Rights', Final Report submitted by the Special Rapporteur, UN Doc. E/CN.4/Sub.2/1992/16, para.98.

91   Felice, W., *supra* n.29, 24.

92   Kaul, I., Grunberg, I. and Stern, M. (eds) (1999), *Global Public Goods: International Cooperation in the 21st Century* (Oxford University Press).

93   Felice, W., *supra* n.29, 23.

94   Vierdag, E. (1973), *The Concept of Discrimination in International Law* (The Hague: Martinus Nijhoff), 7 and 17-8.

95   Sen, A. (1999), *Development as Freedom* (Oxford University Press), 3-13.

such functions through education, rule of law, healthcare, public infrastructure and cultural protections.[96]

These instrumental elements of the development process are essential for attaining human rights entitlements. Their fulfillment makes living possible.[97] These undertakings for the public good are generally assumed to be obligations governed by public policy. Is the state still able to regulate in order to promote public goods, equality and capability through economic, social and cultural rights in an era of economic globalization? Economic globalization has diminished the state's ability to control economic outcomes that directly influence the provision of these rights. Yet states remain the central actors in economic planning. Citizens and states are under a legal obligation to support policies, institutions, and agencies that fulfill these social needs. This requires ensuring that all relevant actors respect these norms.

State economic planning has put in place investment protection treaties that challenge the fulfillment of human rights obligations. Attempts to ensure that private investors' infrastructure projects operate in a manner conducive to human rights goals may be difficult to enact, as these investors are protected from performance requirements by bilateral treaties. For example, in South Africa and Malaysia, attempts have been made to ensure the participation of minority groups in major infrastructural projects.[98] These attempts at governmental regulation of the private sector have resulted in threats of litigation and potential challenges under various investment agreements.[99]

Of all the provisions contained in bilateral investment treaties, the most controversial and troublesome are those dealing with expropriation and performance requirements. The notion of indirect expropriation conflicts with governmental regulations for the public purpose. Expropriation provisions require that domestic regulations be as limited as possible so as not to impact on investors' rights. Parochial interpretation of investment treaties can reduce governmental regulatory space.[100] In determining the existence of indirect expropriation, investor-state dispute resolution mechanisms consider the impact of government policy on investment above concerns of public purpose and human rights law.[101]

States have used available policy space to build a domestic political consensus around economic and social policies, to direct foreign capital to social and environmental ends, to address long-standing social inequalities, and to deal with

---

96   *Ibid.*

97   Dasgupta, P. (1993), *An Inquiry into Well-Being and Destitution* (Oxford University Press), 40 and 54.

98   The situation in South Africa is developed in detail in Chapter 3.

99   Cho, A. and Dubash, N. (5 Sept 2003), 'Will Investment Rules Shrink Policy Space for Sustainable Development? Evidence from the Electricity Sector' (World Resources Institute Working Paper), 29-34 (published online <www.iisd.org/pdf/2003/trade_investment_rules. pdf>, accessed 11 March 2008).

100   Schneiderman, D. (2000), 'Investment Rules and the New Constitutionalism', *Law and Social Inquiry* 25, 767.

101   See *Metalclad Corp. v. Mexico*, Final Award, 2 Sept 2000, Case No. ARB(AF)/97/1, para.111; *Pope and Talbot v. Canada*, Interim Award on Merits, 26 June 2000, para.102 (available online <www.dfait-maeci.gc.ca/tna-nac/pope-en.asp>, accessed 11 March 2008).

external shocks.[102] It is unclear what amounts to indirect expropriation in disputes where the government is regulating in favour of clear public policy. This confusion is detrimental to the promotion of a rights-based approach to development. Developing states may be forced to pay compensation to private companies in disputes even if disputed regulation is clearly within the public interest. This type of deterrent ensures that governments may take investors' rights into account before enacting any legislation.

Public policy concerning the provision of instrumental services depends on the ability of governments to ensure access and quality. National development should require the reduction of poverty through a participatory, empowering and accountable framework. These policy objectives could be in direct conflict with the investment protection regime. Equality-based subsidy programmes or preference policies are very difficult to impose upon private investors.[103] Governments, not private investors, are responsible for the realization of human rights law within the development process.

The poor will not feel the benefits of investment unless states are willing and able to regulate in their favour. This requires investment in infrastructure and a commitment to economic stability. Investment regulation requires commitments to advancing the capabilities of the poor and marginalized groups within society. This includes: human capital investments in health and education; business capital and infrastructure such as transportation, water and ports; natural capital such as biodiversity and healthy soils; public institutional capital, including commercial law, judicial systems, government services and policing; and knowledge capital, which refers to the scientific and technological know how required to raise productivity.[104] Foreign investment does not target these areas specifically unless they constitute sound short-term investments guaranteeing favourable returns.

Action is required at the national level. States must engage with foreign investment in a rights-based manner addressing more than just market interests.[105] Developing states must take human rights seriously and divert resources toward their fulfillment. This would allow for development programmes to be established according to unique domestic requirements. The second phase of capacity building must be accompanied by international cooperation bilaterally, regionally or internationally. Developed states must move beyond the promotion of investment and political rhetoric to deliver on their commitments to human rights.

Economic Globalization as Development

Foreign investment and its legal protection is central to development. Both international investment and the human rights movements entail positive obligations

---

102   Cho A. and Dubash, N., *supra* n.99.
103   Schneiderman, D., *supra* n.100, 767.
104   Sachs, J. (2005), *The End of Poverty: Economic Possibilities in Our Times* (Penguin), 244.
105   De Feyter, K. (2005), *Human Rights: Social Justice in the Age of the Market* (Zed Books), 20-1.

for states. However, they have competing concepts of the role of the state. Economic globalization reduces the role of the state. This is due to the belief that government interference in the free market process impedes economic growth.[106] Thus, the debate surrounding the development process centres on the appropriate role for the state and the market. A state that attempts regulation in favour of rights-based national programmes risks legal action and political estrangement from investors and their home-states.

Donnelly has argued that, 'human rights and sustainable human development "are inextricably linked" only if development is defined to make this relationship tautological'.[107] Currently, development policy centres on the facilitation of foreign investment, or in other words, increased globalization. Low levels of development assistance coupled with foreign investment cannot replace multilateral action to establish a just and democratic international order.[108] The net average share of gross domestic product directed towards social policy has fallen as developing states embrace neoliberal policies in competition for foreign investment.[109] Social policy is seen as undermining market discipline and adversely affecting competitiveness.

Economic globalization is now development. Economic globalization is essentially about expanding capitalist operations through investment into previously underdeveloped markets.[110] This implies moving or creating at least some economic activity in the developing world. The investment project has become the priority of the international community, highlighting the relative weakness of the human rights project. Developing states have flocked to join the global economy by reducing barriers to trade and investment.[111] This has increased the ability of dominant states to influence national policies of developing states in order to further their own private sectors.[112] Theories concerning development have focussed on this type of globalization long before the term became fashionable.[113]

Development theories of imperialism, modernization, dependency and modes of production apply to globalization.[114] Theories of imperialism focus on monopolistic

---

106   Friedman, M. (1982), *Capitalism and Freedom* (University of Chicago Press); Dillard, D. (1992), 'Capitalism', in Wilber, C. and Jameson, K. (eds), *The Political Economy of Development and Underdevelopment* (New York: Mcgraw-Hill), 85-93.

107   Donnelly, J. (1999), 'Human Rights, Democracy and Development', *Human Rights Quarterly* 21.2, 611.

108   Report of the working group on the right to development on its 3rd session (28 Feb-8 March 2002), 'Right to Development', UN Doc. E/CN.4/2002/28/Rev.1, para.52,d.

109   Rudra, N. (2002), 'Globalization and the Decline of the Welfare State in Less-Developed Countries', *International Organization* 56.2, 411.

110   Stiglitz, J. (2003), *Globalization and Its Discontents* (New York: W.W. Norton and Co.), 7.

111   For criticism, see Falk, R. (1999), *Predatory Globalization* (Cambridge: Polity Press).

112   Alston, P. (1998), 'The Universal Declaration in an Era of Globalization', in Heijden B. and Tahzi-Lie, B. (eds), *Reflections on the Universal Declaration of Human Rights: A Fiftieth Anniversary Anthology* (The Hague: Martinus Nijhoff, 1998), 29.

113   Sklair, L., *supra* n.62, 29.

114   *Ibid.* p.30.

international capitalism, which is associated with economic globalization. International capitalism has been analysed by Marxist scholars such as Lenin, who famously interpreted capitalism in an international context as imperialism.[115] Lenin's analysis emphasizes state-centric economic neo-imperialism. Modernization theories revolve around the necessity to refashion traditional societies and include them in a global capitalist economic system. Traditional societies are viewed as inhibiting such progress and must evolve along a set path towards an ideal of modernity based on the Western state model.[116]

Dependency theory is the most influential neo-Marxist analysis of international development.[117] According to this persistently relevant theory, the centre (the developed industrial states) uses the periphery (the underdeveloped majority of states) to supply resources in order to fuel markets. No genuine development is possible as long as a dependent relationship predominates. The best a dependent relationship can produce is enclave development, which reproduces the dependent relationship domestically and regionally.[118] These theories of development, alongside the resurgent laissez-faire neoliberal doctrine, are analogous with the current debates on globalization. Sklair's point, that globalization is nothing new but just sped up due to increased technological advances,[119] seems appropriate.

Neoliberal reform is the backbone of economic globalization. Stiglitz explains in the context of Latin America that: 'The question that is being debated in Latin America is whether reform has failed Latin America or globalization has failed Latin America. In some sense, though, those two issues are really the same, because a key part of the reform agenda was globalization'.[120] Development is now tautological with globalization instead of human rights.

This self-imposed reduction of state autonomy over national decision making is a product of dependent economic relationships. This implicates dominant states in the creation of an international system that puts investment first. Many economists insist that economic globalization is entirely positive in terms of development. It is suggested that mutual interdependence and common interests necessitate stability and peace.[121] However, this interdependence is not often symmetrical as trade, investment and markets can operate within or even create uneven power relations

---

115   See Lenin, V. (1917), *Imperialism, The Highest Stage of Capitalism* (published in pamphlet form, Petrograd).

116   Sklair, L., *supra* n.62, 32.

117   *Ibid.*

118   *Ibid.*, 33.

119   *Ibid.*, 29.

120   Stiglitz, J. (2003), 'Globalization and Development', in Held, D. and Koenig-Archibugi, M. (eds), *supra* n.11, 48.

121   See Dougherty, J. and Pfaltzgraff, R. (2001), *Contending Theories of International Relations: A Comprehensive Survey* (5th edn, New York: Longman), 505-46.

among states.[122] Such power relations can result in the political exploitation of market interdependence.[123]

International relations theory explains that economically powerful states have the capacity to influence policy in other states.[124] This influence is not often wielded for the common good. Economic influence is used to promote national interests.[125] Accordingly, the dominant states (or state) shape globalization to match their interests. Economic globalization/development has not been successful in terms of human rights. It does not have to be that way. Globalization requires management. Stiglitz explains further:

> I believe that globalization – the removal of barriers to trade and the closer integration of national economies – can be a force for good and that it has the potential to enrich everyone in the world, particularly the poor. But I also believe, if this is to be the case, the way globalization has been managed, including the international trade agreements that have played such a large role in removing those barriers and the policies that have been imposed on developing countries in the process of globalization, need to be radically rethought.[126]

The investment protection project is an example of disregarding human rights while promoting globalization. Once investment treaties instill market protections, corporations become increasingly powerful. They gain the capability to pressure states to adopt and retain the corporate agenda both as a domestic interest group and through their connection with the international economic system.[127] Developing states have been convinced to ease labour standards, modify tax regulations, and relax other rules to attract investment.[128]

This structural adjustment can lead to a significant erosion of human rights standards and hamper the ability of countries to independently determine their development priorities.[129] For example, the United Nations Conference on Trade and Development reported that 71 countries made 208 changes in foreign investment laws, with more than 90 per cent enhancing investors' rights while making the investment climate more favourable to foreign investment.[130] However, the vast majority of trade and investment remains exclusively between developed states. Only

---

122   See Hirshman, A. (1969), *National Power and the Structure of Foreign Trade* (University of California Press).

123   This possibility is outlined in detail in the important study by Keohane, R. and Nye, J. (1977), *Power and Interdependence: World Politics in Transition* (Boston: Little Brown and Co.).

124   Goldstein, J., *supra* n.25, 73-8.

125   Gilpin, R., *supra* n.2, 252.

126   Stiglitz, J., *supra* n.110, x.

127   De Feyter, K., *supra* n.105, 12.

128   See Spar, D. and Yoffie, D. (1999), 'Multinational Enterprises and the Prospects for Justice', *Journal of International Affairs* 52, 557.

129   Teeple, G. (2000), *Globalization and the Decline of Social Reform* (Toronto: Garamond Press), 87.

130   United Nations Conference on Trade and Development (UNCTAD) (2002), *World Investment Report: Transnational Corporations and Export Competitiveness* (Geneva).

15 per cent of foreign investment flows from the developed world to the developing, while the largest fraction, worth hundreds of billions of dollars, is concentrated in the United States and Europe.[131] Of the foreign investment made in the developing world, two thirds is concentrated in eight states while half of the developing states in the world receive none.[132] Africa attracted less than 2 per cent of the total foreign investment in 2001.[133] Globalization as development would therefore appear to be a total failure. Nevertheless, the neoliberal leaning of states has resulted globalization and a reduction of the state's capacity and willingness to comply with human rights obligations.[134]

Developing states have less capability and therefore wield less power in terms of shaping the model of economic globalization. In order to develop their economies they must gain capital, which is privately dispersed according to an economic order decided by the national interests of dominant states.[135] This is the root of an economic relationship based upon dependency. Interdependence is prevalent between developed world states while rare in the economic relationships of the developing world to the developed states.[136]

Dependency leads to subservience in policy making which can cause instability. Sachs describes the example of the United States, who requested that the Bolivian government eradicate its farmers' cocoa crops in the 1990s. Bolivia acquiesced, which resulted in the farmers' impoverishment. The Bolivian government then turned to social development programmes as a response, but was unable to afford such plans on their own causing a financial crisis. Foreign investors, international donors and dominant states failed to assist in any meaningful way. The result was civil and political disorder, and riots. The government fell and Bolivia became an unstable society for foreign investment.[137] This is but one of many examples emerging from developing states where domestic populations have grown tired of internationalist government policy that seems insulated from their needs.

Developing states depend upon foreign investment. It is now the main source of capital, reaching twice the official development aid figure by the year 2001.[138] The lack of capital means that states are unable to invest in basic infrastructural developments or in improved factories, farms, mines or oil wells. Foreigners invest in countries and subsequently own the facilities, controlling business decisions that affect the development of local populations. These corporations repatriate

---

131 Gilpin, R., *supra* n.16, 6.

132 United Nations Development Programme (UNDP) (1997), *Human Development Report 1997* (Oxford), 9.

133 United Nations Conference on Trade and Development (UNCTAD) (2002), *World Investment Report: Transnational Corporations and Export Competitiveness* (Geneva), 23.

134 United Nations Committee on Economic, Social and Cultural Rights (CESCR) (18th session, 27 April-15 May 1998), *Statement on Globalization and Economic, Social and Cultural Rights*, para.5 (Geneva).

135 Mosely, L. (2003), *Global Capital and National Governments* (Cambridge University Press), 52.

136 Nayar, D. (ed.) (2002), *Governing Globalization* (Oxford University Press), 7.

137 Sachs, J., *supra* n.104, 79.

138 Goldstein, J., *supra* n.25, 367.

profits, usually to their home-state. Host-states are left with limited taxes and jobs in liberalized sectors of the economy. The ability of foreign investment to infuse capital has been considered to outweigh fears of neo-colonialism and inequality by state decision makers.[139]

This dependence of the developing state on the developed state for investment means that linkage to the global economy requires accepting economic decisions made by developed states. Such decisions ensure an investment system designed to protect the property of the investors headquartered in the home-state. In the case of foreign investment, which lacks an international organization to govern its activities, the relationship is bilateral, a level in which the relationship is at its most unequal.[140]

The reduced role of governments has accentuated the need for human rights law. State economies are complex and require more than just foreign investment.[141] Developing states need infrastructural investment in areas that may not attract foreign investment. Examples of infrastructural development requiring governmental regulation include transportation, power grids, communications, law enforcement, health, education and national defense. These require funds from taxation and public investment in order to function.[142] Yet political will to regulate, at both the national and international level, in favour of social policy in sectors dominated by foreign investment is absent.

Neoliberal reforms advocated by the international community focus on a narrow range of issues, particularly corruption, barriers to private enterprise, budget deficits and state ownership. These involve uniform prescriptions of belt-tightening, trade and investment liberalization and privatization with little regard to particular problems of particular states.[143] For example, common developmental issues such as poverty traps, agronomy, climate, disease, transport, gender issues and lack of economic, social and cultural rights that undermine development are overlooked.[144]

Many developing states struggle to maintain control, as they are often less powerful than the corporations responsible for foreign investment. Developing states have mercantilist fears for the protection of their own economy, as investors are perceived as embodying the national interests of their home-states in the developed world. This reflects the historical fact that most foreign direct investment was conducted in the colonial context as well as the contemporary context of dependency. Despite the fact that capital is a scarce resource required by developing states, they fear the loss of culture, traditional ways of life and exploitation. For these reasons attempts to regulate foreign direct investment remain.[145]

---

139 *Ibid.*
140 Nayar, D. (ed.), *supra* n.136, 7.
141 Sachs, J., *supra* n.104, 74.
142 *Ibid.*, 79.
143 *Ibid.*
144 *Ibid.*
145 See further Mosely, L., *supra* n.135.

Foreign Investment and Development: Positive and Negative Views

Self interest motivates foreign direct investment.[146] Corporations invest in developing states due to a possibility of high returns on their investment. Investors are encouraged by abundant natural resources, geographical location and cheap labour. Financial stability and projected economic growth in the host-state both attract investment. Corporations are attracted to favourable regulatory environments in which the state facilitates their activities.[147] However, basing the prime transfer of capital from the developed to the developing world on profit potential separates it from human rights. Although investment and growth are essential to international development, human rights are essential to providing the equality and stability that facilitates such growth. There is a business oriented link between investment's need for stability and infrastructure and the human rights.

Discourse surrounding development and economic globalization hinges on ideological assumptions. The positive view of economic globalization and development subscribes to neo-classical economic theory. It holds that economic growth is the tide that lifts all boats. Proponents argue that unregulated markets best allocate resources. Therefore, further liberalization should be pursued. Eventually, profits will trickle down to all sectors of society.

The negative view of economic globalization and development is less optimistic about markets. Opponents of globalization as development are concerned with inequality and exploitation. They insist that there remains an unequal economic playing field between developed and developing states.[148] This group is further divided into liberals and more radical Marxist-influenced groups. The liberals believe the market is important for growth but requires regulation to protect against market failure. Marxist-influenced groups distrust the market completely and call for alternative forms of development. This debate between the positive and negative assessments of economic globalization is vital. If the positive view holds, regulation and reform are unnecessary. If the negative view is more relevant, then reform is required urgently.

Positive View   The logic of the positive view is straightforward. The harmonization of standards concerning investment is for the benefit of the international community. It facilitates the operations of corporations. Corporations are the agents of economic globalization. They perform the functions central to globalization defined as the, 'integration of national economies into the international economy through trade, direct foreign investment (by corporations and multinationals), short term capital flows,

---

146   Mosely, L., *supra* n.135, 2-5.
147   Gargan, E. (15 Aug 1992), 'India's Rush to a Free Economy Stumbles', *The New York Times*, 2.
148   Stiglitz, J. (2006), *Making Globalization Work* (New York: W.W. Norton and Co.), 56.

international flows of workers and humanity generally, and flows of technology'.[149] This process is crucial to economic growth and therefore development.[150]

Economic globalization, when combined with democratic internationalism, will lead to 'longer and more sustained peace, longer and more sustained economic growth, and a fairer and better society'.[151] Human rights form but one aspect of a harmonious whole that is best achieved by economic liberalization and increased cooperation between states.[152] Economic growth has brought higher living standards and scientific and technological advances to the world that was not imaginable two centuries ago. Globalization and technology create an even playing field on which developed and developing states compete on equal terms.[153] Living standards are higher than they were at the start of this process in all parts of the world, other than disease-ravaged Africa.[154]

Proponents laud liberalization and harmonization. It is believed that the system instils rationality, objectivity and transparency into international economic relations. This replaces the irrational passion and deference to special interests associated with national governance. Supporters insist globalization will 'secure transparent, stable and predictable conditions for long-term cross-border investment, particularly [foreign direct investment] that will contribute to the expansion of trade'.[155] From this perspective, investment agreements reduce the scope for arbitrary, capricious and economically unsound government policy, providing investors with more certainty and guarantees against risk.

Modern economic growth has also brought phenomenal gaps between the richest and poorest. However, gaps were impossible when poverty gripped the whole world.[156] Overall, economic growth is beneficial although some regions seem to grow slower. The failure of economic globalization to directly cause human rights, justice and equality to materialize is justified by reference to Rawls' philosophy; national failures to implement a programme of good governance are to blame. Developing states that have not benefited from economic globalization have implemented a set of institutions founded on bad domestic policy, corruption and generally bad governance. Rawls indicates that developing state human rights failures are due exclusively to national factors:

---

149 Bhagwati, J. (2004), *In Defense of Globalization* (Oxford University Press), 3.

150 De Schutter, O., *supra* n.1, 404.

151 Moore, M. (2003), *World Without Walls: Freedom, Development, Free Trade and Global Governance* (Cambridge University Press), 249–50.

152 Alvarez, J. (2002), 'The WTO as Linkage Machine', *American Journal of International Law* 96, 146.

153 Friedman, T. (2005), *The World is Flat: A Brief History of the Twenty-First Century* (New York: Farrar, Struas and Giroux).

154 Sachs, J., *supra* n.104, 49.

155 Adlung. R. (2000), 'Services Trade Liberalization from Developed and Developing Country Perspectives', in Sauvé, P. and Stern, R. (eds), *GATS 2000: New Directions in Services Trade Liberalization* (Washington, DC: Brookings Institution Press).

156 Sachs, J., *supra* n.104, 49.

The problem is commonly the nature of the public political culture and the religious and philosophical traditions that underlie its institutions. The great social evils in poor societies are likely to be oppressive government and corrupt elites.[157]

The only method for developing states to escape from such poor governance is to institute structural adjustment policies in political and economic institutions. This reduces the ability of governments to interfere with and distort market forces. Positivist economic arguments show the success of the global economic system. Economic growth enhances human rights by increasing economic benefits and consequent political freedoms.[158] Human rights considerations are excluded from investment agreements, which maintain a technical focus. Success is measured in terms of economic growth rather than through wide ranging rights-based action.

Thus, sustained global economic growth promoted by neoliberal economics is unprecedented and will provide the funds for the realization of human rights.[159] The argument alleges that world poverty and income inequality have been reduced over the past two decades as a result of liberalization policies. Wolf elucidates that, 'evidence suggests the 1980s and 1990s were decades of declining global inequality and reductions in the proportion of the world's population in extreme poverty'.[160] According to the World Bank, 'Over the past 20 years the number of people living on less than 1 dollar a day has fallen by 200 million after rising steadily for 200 years.'[161]

It is assumed that growth leads directly to improvements in social justice, poverty alleviation and increased equality during development. The neoliberal argument claims that justice and equality are results of economic growth. Mahajan responds to critics of this approach as follows:

> Openness to trade and investment, on average, contributes to increasing a country's per-capita growth rate and alleviating its poverty situation, and has no significant relationship with inequality in the country. In sum, globalization is good for growth; growth is good for the poor; globalization has no effect on inequality; hence, globalization is good for the poor. This is a simple yet forceful fact-based conclusion, and cannot be disproved by specific examples to the contrary; any such example could be countered by more examples

157   Rawls, J. (1993), 'The Law of Peoples', in Shute, S. and Hurley, S. (eds), *On Human Rights* (New York: Basic Books), 77.

158   Shelton, D., *supra* n.53, 293.

159   *Ibid.*

160   Wolf, M. (8 May 2002), 'Doing More Harm than Good', *Financial Times*; see also: Wolf, M. (19 Dec 2001), 'Stepping Stone from Poverty', *Financial Times*; Wolf, M. (8 Feb 2000), 'The Big Lie of Global Inequality', *Financial Times*.

161   World Bank (2002), *World Development Indicators 2002* (Washington D.C.: World Bank); Many analysts claim inequality has fallen in the last 20 years. For example, see Ormerod, P. (Aug/Sept 2000), 'Inequality: The Long View', *Prospect*; Wright, R. (Dec 2000), 'Global Happiness', *Prospect*; Wolf, M. (24 Jan 2001), 'Growth Makes the Poor Richer', *Financial Times*.

where globalization works for the benefit of the poor. Passionate discourses do not tell the broader truth: factual statements do![162]

Privatization and deregulation have positive practical effects such as increased provision and efficiency of services. The liberalization of investment in services facilitates investment flows across borders. This enables economic actors to respond to new types of demand. It can provide levels of service that are difficult for developing states to achieve alone.[163] This lowers costs and opens up opportunities for entrepreneurs. Liberalization makes business more profitable creating employment. This process should enhance human capital by providing access to services that contribute to the fulfillment of human rights.[164]

Inconsistencies within the world investment system will be overcome with time through economic growth. It is contended that the oft-mentioned income gap between and within states was probably lessened by global investment, at least in the states that are integrated into the global economy. By opening up to investment, developing states have lowered this inequality. A fully integrated world economy has lower inequality than a segmented one.[165]

Investment liberalization and expansion are helpful for developing political freedom and the rule of law which are necessary for the enjoyment of human rights. This system allows for individuals to pursue self-interest that raises the standard of living for all. Internationally, this system promotes interdependence between states and provides incentives to join in a stable and secure system. Economic enticement can be used to sanction human rights abusing countries by excluding them from the benefits of investment. The argument is mirrored in the discussion of free trade. In this context, Bello explains that:

> Trade liberalization promotes the growth of stability-promoting middle class all over the globe; trade enhances efficiency and wealth and thereby creates potential revenue for environmental protection. Trade creates jobs in developing as well as developed countries, thereby reducing the pressure on both illegal immigration and illicit drug trafficking. Trade liberalization is not a panacea for the world's problems, but it can be part of a solution for many of them.[166]

The philosophy of Rawls is convincingly used to support this logic. Rawls' philosophy of social justice provides that social and economic inequality is admissible as long as it benefits the least advantaged members of society.[167] Thus, social justice requires incentives to capital because the lack thereof would harm the economy. Hampering economic growth has negative consequences for the least advantaged members of

---

162   World Bank economist Sandeep Mahajan, quoted in Mendes, E. and Mehmet, O. (2003), *Global Governance, Economy and Law: Waiting for Justice* (London: Routledge Studies in International Law), 76.

163   Koenig-Archibugi, M., *supra* n.89, 5.

164   Jameson, K. and Wilber, C. (eds), *supra* n.106, 433.

165   Mendes, E. and Mehmet, O., *supra* n.162, 77.

166   Bello, J. (1996), 'National Sovereignty and Transnational Problem Solving', *Cardozo Law Revue* 18, 1029.

167   See Rawls, J. (1971), *A Theory of Justice* (Harvard University Press).

society. The contemporary system of investment liberalization provides investment opportunities in developing states. Investment is vital because it is the main source of capital. Sovereign states accept the conditions of investment as they realize that this competitiveness will ensure investment and bring economic growth. Rising levels of inequality associated with market forces are excusable in order to elevate overall poverty.[168]

Negative View   This optimistic view of globalization as development is not the consensus. The negative view of economic globalization is a more nuanced one. It is uncertain that globalization promotes the common good and therefore human rights.[169] While some net benefits may be positive, they are distributed unevenly. Inequalities between and within states are the result of barriers to development occurring in developing states. For example, in the past, many developing states faced brutal exploitation by dominant colonial powers. They still must overcome geographical barriers including those related to climate, food production, disease, energy resources and proximity to markets that did not burden early industrializing states.[170]

Marginalization can only be overcome through the practical application of planned policy making and infrastructural development.[171] Joining the competition for international investment may not be enough. The situation in the least developed states remains unpromising.[172] Despite reassurances to the contrary, the last decade of the twentieth century saw an increase of one hundred million people living in poverty.[173] This occurred simultaneously with annual world economic growth of 2.5 per cent.[174] Approximately 20 per cent of the world lives on less than one dollar per day and 50 per cent on less than two dollars per day.[175] For the 614 million people living in the least developed countries, there is very little chance of marked improvement in average living standards in the short and medium term despite the fact that most have liberalized their economies.[176]

Investors seem better protected than other people in globalization. Investors have access to dispute resolution mechanisms and have considerable influence over domestic governments, ensuring adherence to the investment project.[177] Investment

168   van Parijs, P. (1995), *Real Freedom for All: What (If Anything) Can Justify Capitalism?* (Oxford University Press), 227.

169   Wade, R. *supra* n.80, 39.

170   Sachs, J., *supra* n.104, 50.

171   *Ibid.*

172   'Right to Development', *supra* n.108, para.32.

173   World Bank (2000), *Global Economic Prospects and the Developing Countries 2000* (Washington D.C.: World Bank), 29.

174   Stiglitz, J., *supra* n.110, 5.

175   *Ibid.*, 47.

176   United Nations Conference on Trade and Development (UNCTAD) (2000), *The Least Developed Countries 2000 Report. Aid, Private Capital Flows and External Debt: The Challenge of Financing Development in the LDCs*, UN Doc. UNCTAD/LDC/2000, Sales No. E.00.II.D.21.

177   Shelton, D., *supra* n.53, 297.

agreements enable profit flight with little left over for domestic human rights programmes.[178] Domestic populations, on the other hand, must rely on governments implementing policy often with no recourse to enforceable arbitration.

Developed states never conformed to the neoliberal model.[179] Developing states should be given an opportunity to develop without investment constraints, which enforce market-based development. This requires a just system of development that recognizes past inequalities and mandates international cooperation to overcome them. Currently, any state regulation that applies to corporations can be considered a barrier to investment. Yet the developed world maintained obstacles to free trade and investment while protecting its industries during its own development.[180] Historically, similar transformations in transportation, communication and technology occurred in the now developed states, creating national markets. During that period, strong central governments financed and controlled development in order to ensure it was beneficial to national interests.[181] Developed states invested heavily in public institutions and created a welfare state.[182] Growing democratization nationally ensured free market economics could not survive without social justice. Even the United States and Britain turned to centrally planned economies in a quest for national autonomy.[183] Galbraith explained that:

> Through the nineteenth century, liberalism in its classical meaning having become the conventional wisdom, there were solemn warnings of the irreparable damage that would be done by Factory Acts, trade unions, social insurance and other social legislation. Liberalism was a fabric, which could not be raveled without being rent. Yet the desire for protection and security and some measure of equality in bargaining power would not down. In the end it became a fact with which the conventional wisdom could not deal. The Webbs, Lloyd George, LaFollette, Roosevelt, Beveridge and others crystallized the acceptance of the new fact. The result is what we call the welfare state.[184]

This compromise reflected a concession to equality and justice in exchange for the acceptance of relatively open markets. Ruggie has stated that: 'Governments played a key role in enacting and sustaining the compromise: moderating the volatility of transaction flows across borders and providing social investments, safety nets and adjustment assistance – yet all the while pushing international liberalization.'[185]

---

178 Shalankany, A., *supra* n.76, 429.

179 Koenig-Archibugi, M., *supra* n.89, 3-4.

180 Jameson, K. and Wilber, C. (eds), *supra* n.106, 91.

181 Stiglitz, J., *supra* n.120, 52.

182 Wilhelm Scharpf, F. (1999), *Governing in Europe: Effective and Democratic?* (Oxford University Press), 36.

183 Ruggie, J. (2003), 'Taking Embedded Liberalism Global: The Corporate Connection', in Held D. and Koenig-Archibugi, M. (eds), *supra* n.11, 93; see also: Ruggie, J. (1982), 'International Regimes, Transactions and Change: Embedded Liberalism in the Postwar Economic Order', *International Organization* 36; Polanyi, K. (1994), *The Great Transformation* (Boston: Beacon Press); James, H. (2001), *The End of Globalization: Lessons from the Great Depression* (Harvard University Press).

184 Galbraith, K. (1958), *The Affluent Society* (Cambridge: Riverside Press), 15.

185 Ruggie, J. (2003), *supra* n.183, 94.

There is no current international governance system capable of ensuring a similar approach is taken to globalization. North America and Europe continue to protect their economies from external forces,[186] but this privilege does not extend to the developing world.

Corporations thrive most in highly regulated North America and Europe.[187] These states actively invested in research and development as well as infrastructure. Corporate growth has often been monopolistic and state assisted by all means at its disposal. State control of economic growth included the use of fiscal and monetary policies, acting as dominant shareholders in corporations, as well as holding national corporations and development joint ventures with the private sector.[188] The state apparatus increased congruently with the growth of corporate capital.[189] Yet, similar attempts to regulate investment can be in direct violation of investment protection treaties in developing states. Stiglitz criticizes this hypocrisy as follows:

> Today, few – apart from those with vested interests who benefit from keeping out the goods produced by the poor countries – defend the hypocrisy of pretending to help the developing countries by forcing them to open up their markets to the goods of the advanced industrial countries while keeping their own markets protected, policies that make the rich richer and the poor more impoverished – and increasingly angry.[190]

The East Asian Tigers are repeatedly lauded as success stories of globalization. Globalization undoubtedly assisted productivity in these states. But these states managed their economies and invested in infrastructure including health and education.[191] Economists do not take into account factors outside of market functions. None of these states operates under perfect competition internationally.[192] The Asian Tiger economies selectively liberalized when it was advantageous and protected when it was not.[193] All gain from geographic proximity to non-capitalist China. Most of these states indirectly benefited from the planned and assisted development of Japan and Korea.[194] They also assured that growth was distributed more evenly, which would not have occurred in unregulated markets.[195]

---

186   Stiglitz, J., *supra* n.120, 56.

187   See United Nations Conference on Trade and Development (UNCTAD) (1999), *World Investment Report, FDI and the Challenge of Development* UN Doc. UNCTAD/WIR/1999, Sales No. E.99.II.D.3; Organization for Economic Cooperation and Development (OECD) (1996), *Trade, Employment and Labour Standards: A Study of Core Workers rights and International Trade* (OECD).

188   Clement, W. (1975), *The Canadian Corporate Elite: An Analysis of Economic Power* (Toronto: McClelland and Stewart), 102; Kirk Laux, J. and Appel Molot, M. (1980), *State Capitalism: Public Enterprise in Canada* (Cornell University Press), 125-50; Olsen, D. (1980), *The State Elite* (Toronto: McClelland and Stewart, 1980), 6-7.

189   Traves, T. (1979), *The State and Enterprise* (University of Toronto Press), 155.

190   Stiglitz, J., *supra* n.110, xv.

191   *Ibid.*, 31.

192   *Ibid.*, 20.

193   *Ibid.*, 60.

194   Wade, R. *supra* n.80, 38-9; Sachs, J., *supra* n.104, 130.

195   Stiglitz, J., *supra* n.148, 31.

None of these conditions applies to developing world states in Africa and South America that are asked to follow the liberalization process, but with no additional funding for social and economic infrastructure.[196] Developing states are not afforded the privilege of regulating the liberalization process. Many lack the institutional capacity and willingness to do so, which has resulted in a failure to exploit the opportunities presented by economic globalization.[197] Without such crucial planning and international assistance, the state is likely to be dominated in a global economy.[198] The global economy requires a sound social and political foundation that necessitates a role for states. Economically successful states have been able to wisely and selectively protect industries in order to build up their economies, for example China, India and Brazil.[199]

States that have followed the Washington Consensus reforms have not been as successful. Shiva explains that long standing human rights values, such as food provisions, health care, education, social security and institutions have been dismantled by states and have then been transformed into corporate monopolies under the guise of competitiveness and efficiency.[200] Citizens and the state pay as corporations extract revenue and capital. This shrinking tax base is felt even in the most developed states, where treasured health and education services are suffering.[201]

During the last decade, political scientists have devoted substantial attention to the role of the state and regulation,[202] attributing unbalanced influence on domestic policy to investment interests.[203] These influential interests can promote dependent relations between states.[204] Once established in states, the influence of investment markets on governmental policy autonomy is especially pronounced in the developing world.[205] Gilpin notes that, 'The inevitable clash between the logic of the market and the logic of the state is central to the study of international political economy.'[206]

---

196   Riddell, B. (1996), 'Things Fall Apart Again: Structural Adjustment Programmes in Sub-Saharan Africa', in Jameson, K. and Wilber, C. (eds), *supra* n.106, 217; Won Chol, D. (1996), 'The Pacific Basin and Latin America', in Jameson, K. and Wilber, C. (eds), *supra* n.106, 384.

197   Ruggie, J. (2003), *supra* n.183, 94.

198   Gilpin, R., *supra* n.16, 304.

199   Stiglitz, J., *supra* n.110, 17.

200   Shiva, V., *supra* n.8, 91.

201   *Ibid.*

202   See Cohen, B. (1996), *In Whose Interest? International Banking and American Foreign Policy* (Yale University Press); Drezner, D. (2001), 'Globalization and Policy Convergence', *International Studies Review* 3, 53; Evans, P. (1997), 'The Eclipse of the State? Reflections on Stateness in an Era of Globalization', *World Politics* 50, 62; Garrett, G (1996), 'Capital Mobility, Trade and Domestic Politics of Economic Policy', in Milner, H. and Keohane, R. (eds), *International and Domestic Politics* (Cambridge University Press).

203   See Block, F. (1997), 'The Ruling Class Does Not Rule: Notes on the Marxist Theory of the State', *Socialist Revolution* 33.

204   See Burtless, G. et al. (1998), *Globaphobia: Confronting Fears about Open Trade* (Washington, D.C.: Progressive Policy Institute and Brookings Institute).

205   Mosely, L., *supra* n.135, 3.

206   Gilpin, R., *supra* n.16, 81.

Human rights, depending on the state for fulfillment, are also inextricably linked to this study.

States often must act against their domestic populations and their commitments to a rights-based development in order to conform to liberalization strategies. For example, state policy promoting regional or gender based development programmes, as advocated by the United Nations, may conflict with neoliberal economic strategy.[207] The ability to compensate through redistribution is sacrificed by states on the domestic and international levels. Public services are reduced to attract investment while the international redistribution to compensate suffers from a lack of political will.[208]

Developing states may not be able to retain institutional capacity sufficient to ensure that all have access to a market-based system.[209] Strong institutional capability for regulation is instrumental in enhancing the positive impact, and limiting the negative impact, of foreign investment. Without this regulation, investment can be harmful to human rights realization. It may not even promote the economic growth it is assumed to create.[210] Investment liberalization can result in positive or negative impacts.[211] One example is the availability and quality of services in the development context is water service privatization in many developing states.[212] Foreign investment should improve quality and access. These services have failed to ensure entitlements and to guarantee that government obligations are fulfilled. Private investors may not deliver services adequately or may do so in an unequal and discriminatory manner.[213] The lack of public infrastructure is an instrumental component of poverty.[214]

The market can be the incorporation of irrational passion, secrecy and singularity, the very aspects of local decision-making which the market-based system was meant to avoid.[215] Orford has eloquently argued that 'this relationship founds an economy of sacrifice, accompanied by the promise of the reward of the righteous in the future by the Father (God/Market) who sees in secret'.[216] Free-market agreements

207   'Role of the United Nations in promoting development in the context of globalization and interdependence', UN Doc. A/RES/60/204 (13 March 2006) (para.18).

208   Koenig-Archibugi, M., *supra* n.89, 7.

209   Wade, R. *supra* n.80, 35-9.

210   Cosbey, A. (2004), *A Capabilities Approach to Trade and Sustainable Development: Using Amartya Sen's Conception of Development to Re-examine the Debates* (Switzerland: International Institute for Sustainable Development), 4.

211   Wade, R. *supra* n.80, 39.

212   See Vaughan, S. (2003), 'Privatisation, Trade Policy and the Question of Water', Les séminaires de l'Iddri No. 9. (Paris: Institut de Dévelopment Durable et des Relations Internationales).

213   See Watkins, K. and Fowler, P. (2002), *Rigged Rules and Double Standards: Trade Globalization and the Fight against Poverty* (Oxfam Campaign Report).

214   See Narayan, D. (2000), *Voices of the Poor: Can Anyone Hear Us?* (Oxford University Press).

215   Orford, A. (2005), 'Beyond Harmonization: Human Rights and the Economy of Sacrifice', in *Leiden Journal of International Law* 18, 182.

216   *Ibid.*

insist that parties sacrifice the linkage to human rights law in the competition for capital amongst a 'community of believers'.[217] When non-believing states, such as Venezuela, Brazil and Bolivia, have attempted to redistribute wealth through health and education to the poor, they have been labeled as populist.[218]

The problem of globalization is inequality. Many integrated states have improved their gross domestic product but have suffered an increased income gap within their countries. A state with improved gross domestic product may still have populations dislocated from human rights entitlements.[219] Economic growth is not often uniformly distributed.[220] Growth may enrich those linked to good market opportunities but bypass the poorest in the same community. In almost all developing states that have rapidly liberalized, inequality has increased while employment levels have declined.[221] Social expenditure is required to lift marginalized groups from poverty amidst economic growth.[222]

Demanding regulations could result in the withdrawal of support by international financial institutions such as the World Bank and the International Monetary Fund.[223] This would cause capital flight and destroy the chances of economic growth in many states. The market, in this view, is not the sole answer to human development:

> What is clear is that open, well-functioning markets need not produce convergence between parts of the low income zone and the high-income zone, and can produce divergence, polarization; which underlines the need for non-market measures of intervention if sizable fractions of the world's population are to catch up in living standards over the next half century or so.[224]

Avenues must be sought and discovered that ensure the ability and the duty of states to perform critical functions. Economic growth is essential to development and the alleviation of poverty, but the state must retain its ability to guarantee human rights. Conclusions that poverty is still rampant internationally and that inequality is rising both within states and internationally point toward the need for alternative development strategies.[225] Economic globalization can be a force for good but it is not a panacea, despite the progress attributed to it. Wade asserts that, 'We should not accept the commonly heard assertion that widening world income inequality is not

---

217   *Ibid.*

218   Stiglitz, J., *supra* n.148, 37.

219   Türk, D. (1994), 'Development and Human Rights', in Henkin, L. and Hargrove, J. (eds), *Human Rights: An Agenda for the Next Century* (Washington D.C.: The American Society for International Law), 167-73.

220   Mendes, E. and Mehmet, O., *supra* n.162, 77.

221   United Nations Conference on Trade and Development (UNCTAD) (1997), *Trade and Development Report. Globalization: Distribution and Growth*, UN Doc. UNCTAD/TDR/17, Sales No. E.97.II.D.8.

222   Sachs, J., *supra* n.104, 72.

223   Wade, R. *supra* n.80, 39.

224   *Ibid.*

225   *Ibid.*, 40.

a negative provided that real indicators like life expectancy are improving and the proportion living in extreme poverty is going down.'[226]

Corporations and Development

The global economy has given rise to non-state actors beyond the complete state control. Increasing attention has been focused on non-state actors in recent years.[227] Non-state actors include a wide range of organizations from multinational corporations to armed resistance groups.[228] Development discourse is concerned primarily with corporations and their activities that challenge the fulfillment of human rights law.[229]

The multinational corporation is a non-state actor that does business with, and invests in, numerous states.[230] Some of these corporations have larger economies than many states.[231] The largest fifteen corporations have revenues greater than all but thirteen nations.[232] The trend remains toward greater corporate dominance. Corporations operate internationally and control the majority of trade and investment. This directly shapes the daily lives of people around the world, yet there is relatively little governmental supervision.[233]

---

226   *Ibid.*, 41.

227   E.g. Alston, P. (ed.), *supra* n.56; Oloka-Onyango, J. (2003), 'Reinforcing Marginalized Rights in the Age of Globalization: Non-State Actors and the Struggle for Peoples' Rights in Africa', *American University International Law Review* 18; Schabas, W. (2003), 'Theoretical and International Framework: Punishment of Non-State Actors in Non-International Armed Conflict', *Fordham International Law Journal* 26; Kamminga, M. and Zia Zarifi, S. (eds), *supra* n.72; Paust, J. (1992), 'The Other Side of Right: Private Duties Under Human Rights Law', *Harvard Human Rights Journal* 5; Jochnick, C., *supra* n.45; Richard Higgot, et al. (eds), *Non-State Actors and Authority in the Global System* (2000); Bas Arts, Maths Noorman and Bob Reinalda (eds), *Non-State Actors in International Relations* (Aldershot, 2001); Bas Arts. 'Non-State Actors in Global Governance: Three Faces of Power', in *Max Planck Project Group on Common Goods* (Bonn: Working Paper 2003/4); De Feyter, K., *supra* n.105; De Feyter K. and Gomez I. (eds), *supra* n.22.

228   On the confusing definition of non-State actors see the interesting discussion in: Phillip Alston. 'The 'Not-a-Cat' Syndrome: Can the International Human Rights Regime Accommodate Non-State Actors?' in Alston, P. (ed.), *supra* n.56, 3-4 and 14-19.

229   Other important non-State actors are Non-Governmental Organizations (NGOs) and Intergovernmental Organizations (IGOs). Both are influential and important in the context of globalization, governance and human rights but are not the subject of this book.

230   The term corporation will be used here to denote all types of transnational or multinational corporations as well as transnational or multinational enterprises.

231   See Global Policy Forum (10 May 2000), *Comparison of Revenues Among States and TNCs* (available online <http://www.globalpolicy.org/socecon/tncs/tables/tncstat2.htm>, accessed 12 March 2008).

232   *Ibid.*

233   See Clausing, K. (2001), 'The Behavior of Intra-firm Trade Prices in U.S. International Price Data', United States Department of Labor, Bureau of Labor Statistics (Washington D.C.: BLS Working Paper 333).

Two aspects of corporate activity are prominent regarding human rights and development. First, corporations can violate human rights in conjunction with states or independently without state action.[234] Second, economic globalization empowers corporations and increases their influence on state regulation through the expansion of foreign investment. Although not in direct control, the corporation exercises important influence over human rights policy.[235] Corporate operations impact the economic welfare of surrounding communities affecting the realization of human rights.[236]

A number of significant cases have displayed the direct connection between corporations and human rights violations. Among the most prominent are Shell in Ogoniland,[237] British Petroleum in Columbia[238] and Unocal in Myanmar.[239] These cases have alerted civil society prompting calls for direct human rights accountability of the corporation.[240] The indirect consequences for human rights in the sphere of development caused by the influence of corporations are even more important. Corporate activity influences framework in which all human rights must be realized and limits the ability of states to enact positive obligations. This interferes with state responsibility for the right to development.

Increasingly, human rights advocates in civil society are abandoning the state as the mediator between international law and non-state actors.[241] The concept of responsibility accompanying power logically leads to demands upon the corporation. Although the traditional view of human rights law concerns the relationship between the state and the individual, increasing attention has been focused on private actors and their effect on human rights. Private actors have duties under international law. This has been confirmed through judicial decisions and treaty interpretation, and highlighted by academic commentators.[242]

The corporation is an established and adaptable entity. It benefits from the doctrine of neoliberal economics as well as the home and host-state quagmire. This advantage combines with limited liability and decentralized decision-making to allow

---

234   Phillipe Robe, J. (1997), 'Multinational Enterprises: The Constitution of a Pluralistic Legal Order', in Teubner G. (ed.), *supra* n.44, 49. Skogly, S. (1999), 'Economic and Social Human Rights, Private Actors and International Obligations', in Addo, M. (ed.), *supra* n.24, 240-41.

235   Muchlinski, P. (2002), 'Human Rights and Multinationals: Is there a Problem?' in *International Affairs* 77, 43.

236   *Ibid.*

237   See Human Rights Watch (1995) *Nigeria, The Ogoni Crisis: A Case Study in Military Oppression in South East Nigeria* (New York: Human Rights Watch), Skogly, S. (1997), 'Complexities in Human Rights Protection: Actors and Rights involved in the Ogoni Conflict in Nigeria', *Netherlands Quarterly on Human Rights* 1, 47-60.

238   'BP Accused of Funding Columbian Death Squads', *The Observer* (20 Oct 1996), I.16.

239   *Doe v. Unocal.* US Dist. Ct., C.D. Cal. 31 Aug 2000, 2000 US Dist. LEXIS 13327.

240   Muchlinski, P., *supra* n.235, 31-2.

241   Reinisch, A., *supra* n.56, 74.

242   Paust, J., *supra* n.227, 51.

for double standards in human rights promotion to take place internationally.[243] The policies of the international economic institutions such as the International Monetary Fund, the World Bank, and the World Trade Organization have allowed corporations to gain even more influence on the development agendas of states.[244]

The corporation's powerful and influential position within the international community gives rise to contradictory capabilities. This position can be used to promote or undermine the realization of human rights in development.[245] Corporate priorities are not equivalent to those of human rights obligations. Corporate priorities are, 'driven essentially by profit, use the smallest number of workers possible, move from jurisdiction to jurisdiction with relative ease, import labour to the detriment of local labour, and they do not always take into account the social needs of the country in which they are operating'.[246] Private investors can ignore policy designed to promote a rights-based approach.[247]

Human rights require special promotion and protection during development[248] but there is a lack of governance at the global level. Stiglitz has summed up undemocratic economic globalization as follows:

> The absence of democratic structures has resulted in trade rules and other rules that are unfair, in which policies tend more to reflect corporate and financial interests than the interests of developing countries and the global economy more generally. The discrepancy between the rhetoric of the advanced industrial countries, including the rules that they fight so strongly for, exposes the developing countries to charges of hierocracy, and undermines confidence in the whole process of globalization.[249]

Existing state obligations for human rights require contemplation in light of the changing nature of international relations. The corporation has not simply wrested power away from the state. Governments have shifted vital components of their functioning to international organizations and private corporations. Corporate involvement in governance has not been limited to the privatization of inefficient national corporations. Services related to human rights once exclusively provided by the state are increasingly being deregulated and privatized.[250] Neoliberal policies

---

243   Addo, M. (1999), 'Human Rights and Transnational Corporations – an Introduction', in Addo, M. (ed.), *supra* n.24, 3; Voon, T. (1999), 'Multinational Enterprises and State Sovereignty under International Law', *Adelaide Law Review* 21, 231.

244   Jagers, N. (1999), 'The Legal Status of the Multinational Corporation Under International Law', in Addo, M. (ed.), *supra* n.24, 259; Tania Voon, 'Multinational Enterprises and State Sovereignty Under International Law', 21 *Adelaide Law Review* (1999), 234-41.

245   'Responsibilities of Transnational Corporations and Other Business Enterprises with Regard to Human Rights', Report of the Sessional Working Group on the Working Methods and Activities of Transnational Corporations. UN Doc. E/CN.4/Sub.2/2002/13., para.5.

246   *Ibid.*

247   Addo, M. (ed.), *supra* n.24, 241.

248   'Responsibilities of Transnational Corporations and Other Business Enterprises with Regard to Human Rights', *supra* n.245, para.12.

249   Stiglitz, J., *supra* n.120, 55.

250   See CCPR Human Rights Committee, 27 July 1995, 'Concluding Observations of the Human Rights Committee: United Kingdom of Great Britain and Northern Ireland', UN

should not decrease the obligation on states to ensure access to important services. Instead of directly providing access, the state must now guarantee that private actors ensure access to such services through supervision and intervention.[251] The changing role of the state, from direct provider to guarantor of services, affects legal frameworks ensuring human rights protection.[252]

States must maintain their prominence as primary duty-holders under international human rights law. This will require states to regulate non-state actors under already existing human rights law. Human rights require promotion as they may inhibit a market-based development programme in the short-run. For this reason, developing states need international cooperation for the regulation of private actors in order to respond effectively to this situation.[253]

Human Rights and Development

The promotion of globalization does not fulfill the cooperative obligations expected of the international community. The fulfillment of human rights, established in principle but not yet implemented, must be part of development. Implementation requires linking development and human rights law in development strategies congruent with human rights norms. State-led industrial and social policy can then help to guide internal development.[254] This may not be in the direct interests of investors.

Developing states must confront globalization and address ongoing violations of human rights. There are realistic expectations on states to implement programmes and institutions designed to protect, promote and fulfill human rights. The state remains the key player in development policy making. The Secretary General of the United Nations has emphasized that:

> Sovereign states are the basic and indispensable building blocks of the international system. It is their job to guarantee the rights of their citizens, to protect them from crime, violence and aggression, and to provide the framework of freedom under law in which individuals can prosper and society develop. If states are fragile, the peoples of the world will not enjoy the security, development and justice that are their right.[255]

Underdevelopment is not an excuse for states to renege on human rights obligations. According to General Comment 3 of the CESCR, lack of economic growth cannot justify a refusal to protect the vulnerable.[256] There is no reason to wait for economic

---

Doc. CCPR/C/79/Add. 55.

251 See De Feyter K. and Gomez I. (eds), *supra* n.22.

252 De Feyter, K., *supra* n.105, 13-5 and 22-3.

253 'Responsibilities of Transnational Corporations and Other Business Enterprises with Regard to Human Rights', *supra* n.245, para.5.

254 See Wade, R. (1990), *Governing the Market* (Princeton University Press).

255 'In Larger Freedom: Towards Development, Security, and Human Rights for All', Report of the Secretary-General, 23 May 2005, UN Doc. A/59/2005, para.19.

256 Committee on Economic, Social and Cultural Rights, 'General Comment 3, The nature of States parties' obligations', 5th session, 1990, UN Doc. E/1991/23, annex III at 86,

growth to fulfill human rights law. It has been shown that the connection between economic growth and human rights protection is tenuous; it is possible to achieve human development even with slow rates of growth.[257] Policies that ensure a process of development based on social services, social safety nets, economic access and social integration can be achieved at low levels of economic growth and with little foreign investment.[258] Policy focused on public services, investment in health and education and affirmative action have assured a human rights foundation for future economic growth.[259]

The connection between human rights law and development is based primarily on rhetorical statements with minimal legal backing. In order to fully integrate human rights law in development, fundamental adjustments of the relationship between individuals and the state, as well as the state and the global economy, are necessary. The Secretary General of the United Nations has stressed that creating an enabling environment for all human rights, including the right to development, requires greater attention.[260] The addition of human rights language to an unjust development system risks preserving inequality.[261] The international community appears to have sidelined the right to development while simultaneously using human rights discourse and promoting foreign direct investment. Economic development itself has been advocated as a new human right, replacing the right to development. In this manner, states and foreign investors can claim they contribute directly to the human right to development.[262]

Economic, Social and Cultural Rights

Civil and political rights have been promoted within development discourse, as they are generally consistent with market-orientated objectives.[263] Civil and political rights are associated with Western values, democracy, the rule of law and the protection of private property. They are perceived as cost-effective and requiring less government intervention, neatly coinciding with the neoliberal agenda.

On the other had, economic, social and cultural rights require positive governmental action.[264] Governments are required to enact appropriate social,

---

para.10-12.

257 Jolly, R. (1997), 'Profiles of Success: Reasons for Hope and Priorities for Action', in Mehrotra, S. and Jolly, R. (eds), *supra* n.37, 8.

258 Streeten, P. et al. (1981), *First Things First: Meeting Basic Needs in Developing Countries* (Oxford University Press), 11.

259 Mehrotra, S., *supra* n.37, 29.

260 UNGA (7 Aug 2003), 'Globalization and its Impact on the Full Enjoyment of All Human Rights', UN Doc. A/58/257, para.7(d)(e).

261 Uvin, P. (2002), 'On Moral high Ground: The Incorporation of Human Rights by the Development Enterprise', *The Fletcher Journal of Development Studies* 27, 3.

262 United Nations Development Programme (UNDP) (1998), *Integrating Human Rights with Sustainable Development, UNDP Policy Document 2*, 6.

263 Jochnick, C., *supra* n.45, 63.

264 International Covenant on Economic, Social and Cultural Rights (adopted 16 Dec 1996, entered into force 3 Jan 1976), G.A. Res. 2200A (XXI), 21 UN GAOR Supp. No. 16 at

economic and political policy in order to ensure their realization.[265] The provision of economic, social and cultural rights requires redistribution of the profits created by economic globalization, both domestically, and internationally through the cooperation of the international community.

Economic, social and cultural rights are the practical basis for achieving a functioning system of interdependent civil and political rights.[266] The lack of economic, social and cultural rights in development affects the majority of the world's population. The collective character of economic, social and cultural rights deepens the volatile nature of the injustice felt. A situation in which economic, social and cultural rights are not implemented renders the exercise of civil and political rights unattainable.[267] Yet, the roots of the violation of economic, social and cultural rights in a globalized world may lie beyond national borders.[268]

Economic, social and cultural rights address social injustice and include rights to nutritional value, clothing, shelter, healthcare, clean water, sanitation, education[269] and can be interpreted to include a sustainable environment.[270] These rights mandate a minimum standard at the national level. Human rights law requires the provision of a framework for ensuring their fulfillment nationally.[271] It has been shown that sufficient resources and knowledge are available globally to ensure this minimum standard. Economic, social and cultural rights require policy geared towards their fulfillment at the national and international levels.[272]

There has been an unacceptable lack of progress in realizing economic, social and cultural rights despite unprecedented international economic growth.[273] Globalization as development ignores the violation of economic, social and cultural rights, while the citizens of developed states enjoy relatively good protection due to past social investment.[274] The prioritization and attainment of a limited civil and political rights agenda in development does not fulfill economic, social and cultural rights obligations.[275]

49, UN Doc. A/6316 (1966), 993 U.N.T.S. 3 (ICESCR).

265　Oloka-Onyango, J., *supra* n.227, 57-60.

266　Agbakwa, S. (2003), 'Economic, Social and Cultural Rights as the Cornerstone of African Human Rights', *Yale University Human Rights and Development Law Journal* 5, 184.

267　*Ibid.*

268　Jochnick, C., *supra* n.45, 56.

269　ICESCR, Part III.

270　Felice, W., *supra* n.29, 38.

271　ICESCR, Article 2 and part IV.

272　Sen, A., *supra* n.95, 108.

273　For example, See Leckie, S. (1989), 'The U.N. Committee on Economic, Social and Cultural Rights and the Right to Adequate Housing: Towards an Appropriate Approach', *Human Rights Quarterly* 11, 525-26.

274　Alves, W. (2000), 'The Declaration of Human Rights in Postmodernity', *Human Rights Quarterly* 22, 485. In this article Alves points out that even in the western world this ethos is eroding rapidly as commitments to economic, social and cultural rights decline internationally.

275　Donnelly, J., *supra* n.107, 612.

The Universal Declaration of Human Rights establishes economic, social and cultural rights as equal to and interdependent with civil and political rights.[276] There is an ideological consensus amongst the international community that human rights are interdependent,[277] yet in practice it is not clear that there is a commitment to this. Economic, social and cultural rights claims must be fundamental, universal and specifiable. In other words, they must guarantee a minimal protection to all regardless of national development. States must ensure a system of accountability to determine whether such rights have been violated or upheld.[278]

Despite the Vienna Declaration and Programme of Action's[279] confirmation of interdependence and universality, the legal protection that states give economic, social and cultural rights is considerably weaker than civil and political rights. Consequently, economic, social and cultural rights are not implemented and do not have enforcement mechanisms.[280] This failure of interdependence has severely limited the progress of human rights law in development. The High Commissioner for Human Rights recognizes this problem and insists that economic, social and cultural rights must be strengthened.[281]

The development of economic social and cultural rights reflected the concern that society should never return to an unregulated capitalist model of economic development.[282] This model had become associated with exploitation and the great depression. National planning for welfare and regulation of the economy was to remain central to policy-making. This contrasted sharply with the liberalization

---

276   Agbakwa, S., *supra* n.266, 177.

277   The Vienna Convention and programme of Action (25 June 1993), United Nations World Conference on Human Rights in Vienna, UN Doc. A/CONF. 157/24 (1993), Section I, para.5, reprinted in 32 International Law Manual 1661 (1993); see also: African Charter of Human and Peoples' Rights (27 June 1981), pmbl., para.8, O.A.U. Doc. CAB/LEG/67/3/Rev. 5 (1982); Proclamation of Tehran (13 May 1969), Final Act of the International Conference on Human Rights, Article 13. UN Doc: A/CONF.32/41 (1968), reprinted in *Human Rights: A Compilation of International Instruments* Vol. I (2nd part), at 51-54 (New York, Geneva: UN), UN Doc. ST/HR/1/Rev.5 (1994); see also: UN ESCOR, Commission on Human Rights (8 Jan. 1987), The Limburg Principles on the Implementation of the International Covenant on Economic, Social and Cultural Rights, princs. 2 and 3, 43rd Sess., Agenda Item 8. UN Doc: E/CN.4/1987/17/Annex (1987), reprinted in 9 *Human Rights Quarterly* (1987), 123; Maastricht Guidelines on Violations of Economic, Social and Cultural Rights, guideline 4, reprinted in 20, *Human Rights Quarterly* (1998), 691 (reemphasizing equality, interdependence and indivisibility of all human rights).

278   Beetham, D. (1995), 'What Future for Economic and Social Rights', in Beetham, D. (ed.), *Politics and Human Rights* (Oxford University Press), 46.

279   The Vienna Convention and Programme of Action (25 June 1993), United Nations World Conference on Human Rights in Vienna, UN Doc. A/CONF. 157/24 (1993), Section I, para.5, reprinted in 32 International Law Manual 1661 (1993).

280   Agbakwa, S., *supra* n.266, 178.

281   High Commissioner for Human Rights, Louise Arbour (26 July 2006), 'Countries Still Giving Lower Priority to Economic, Social and Cultural Rights' (United Nations, Press Release).

282   Muchlinski, P., *supra* n.235, 33

of trade and investment at the heart of the burgeoning global economy.[283] The stratification of human rights discourse emerged on ideological lines. The West, led by the United States, emphasized civil and political rights as the foundation of all rights. The East, led by the Soviet Union, concerned itself primarily with economic, social and cultural rights to the point of justifying the curtailment of civil and political rights in order to achieve them. Anti-colonial politics and the concept of cultural relativism further entrenched this divide.[284]

Human rights discourse was thus conducted under the shadow of the Cold War. This has contributed to the secondary status afforded to economic, social and cultural rights.[285] Economic, social and cultural rights remain contested and are referred to as political aspirations. They are sometimes not considered rights due to legal difficulty associated with determining violations, the identity of the perpetrator and the provision of remedies. Moreover, remedies cost taxpayers money.[286] This 'wooly' social reform is best left to governments.[287] The Economist explains that, 'the most reliable method yet invented to ensure that governments provide people with economic and social necessities is called politics'.[288]

The High Commissioner for Human Rights has stated that, 'this categorization is particularly problematic when considering the links between human rights, security and development which are increasingly recognized'.[289] The Inter-American Court of Human Rights has acknowledged this important link as follows: 'neglect of economic and social rights, especially when political participation has been suppressed, brings about the sort of social polarization that leads, in its turn, to acts of violence by and against the Government'.[290]

Not long ago markets were thought of as imperfect, requiring Keynesian intervention.[291] This concept has been swept aside and qualifications now seem unimportant. Sen ironically comments that any mention of defects in the market system seems terribly old-fashioned.[292] This uncritical enthusiasm for markets has negative consequences for economic social and cultural rights. Conservative voices, such as Michael J. Dennis, an attorney advisor on human rights to the US Department

---

283   Mazower, M. (1999), *Dark Continent: Europe's 20th Century* (Penguin), 206-09.

284   Muchlinski, P., *supra* n.235, 34.

285   Agbakwa, S., *supra* n.266, 177.

286   'Stand Up For You Rights: The old stuffy ones, that is: newer ones are distractions'. *The Economist* (24 March 2007), 12.

287   *Ibid.*

288   *Ibid.*

289   High Commissioner for Human Rights, Louise Arbour (25 Oct 2006), 'Economic and Social Justice for Societies in Transition', Second Annual Transitional Justice Lecture hosted by the Center for Human Rights and Global Justice at New York University School of Law and by the International Center for Transitional Justice' (New York University School of Law, New York) (available online <http://www.chrgj.org/docs/Arbour_25_October_2006. pdf>, accessed 12 March 2008).

290   Inter-American Court of Human Rights (1995), Annual Report (OEA/Ser.L/V.88, Doc. 9 rev. 1, original: Spanish), Chapter IV, part VII.

291   Sen, A., *supra* n.95, 111.

292   *Ibid.*

of state, often insist that economic development through market-based growth is a necessary prerequisite for the realization of human rights:

> From a practical standpoint, it makes little sense to speak of a separate legally enforceable right to food, housing, or medical care when more than one-fifth of the world's population lives on less than $1 a day, and when some 825 million people worldwide do not have enough food to meet their basic nutritional needs today. The solution to the food, housing, and health problems lies in a combination of actions, such as the adoption of national policies for managing natural resources better and expanding trade between surplus and deficit countries, rather than the application of legal sanctions. Alleviating extreme poverty and hunger in any country depends on sustainable and broad-based economic growth and income generation over the long term.[293]

The argument that developing states are too poor to implement economic, social and cultural rights appears to be of merit at first glance. Yet this problem of underdevelopment never seems to affect military expenditure,[294] or prestigious development projects.[295] Furthermore, this presumption is based on the misconception that economic, social and cultural rights are unique in requiring resources and positive action on the part of governments. The provision of all human rights programmes requires funding. For this reason the essential component of development remains resource transfer. Prosperous developed states must be willing to provide funding for rights-based programmes in developing states, but have been reluctant to do so. The right to development would require states to cooperate in order to ensure development that promotes all human rights.

The implication that developing states cannot afford human rights does not make sense in terms of building conditions for economic growth. It is obvious that economic growth requires a healthy, educated and satisfied workforce that does not feel continually exploited and has the capacity to achieve and retain dignity. Development in economic terms relies on having an adaptable, inventive and resourceful working population.[296] This requires investment in education and health like that conducted during the development of post-war Europe, Japan and the late twentieth century East Asian and European economies. These are examples of investment in education, health and infrastructure, which leads to high levels of economic growth.[297]

Human rights discourse may have been divided and misused by powerful vested interests promoting the system of world trade, but many others are adopting the complete human rights mantra on the ground.[298] Challenges to the current system are coming from international civil society and the marginalized populations of the

---

293   Dennis, M. (2002), 'The Justiciability of Economic, Social and Cultural Rights: Entitlements or Empty Promises?' *World Family Forum*, 17.

294   United Nations Development Programme (UNDP) (1990), *Human Development Report 1990*, 4.

295   Agbakwa, S., *supra* n.266, 191.

296   *Ibid.*, 188.

297   See Sen, A., *supra* n.95.

298   Uvin, P., *supra* n.261, 4.

developing world.[299] These views demand the expansion of development policy to include social, economic and cultural rights and corresponding duties to protect, promote and fulfill rights. Critics rebut that these duties are vague, controversial, require unnecessary regulation hampering globalization and dilute the impact of human rights laws as behavioral norms.[300] The Economist asserts that to promote economic, social and cultural rights advocacy is, 'to follow intellectual fashion and dilute the traditional focus on political rights'.[301]

A return to state-led development strategies seems imminent. The states that joined the *laissez faire* Washington Consensus system of development have experienced little or no growth.[302] By contrast, states that tightly controlled their economies and invested in economic, social and cultural progress have experienced rapid growth.[303] The emergence of China as an influential global power and leader of the developing world is a significant indicator of this shift. [304] China claims to concentrate on economic, social and cultural rights citing the need to feed its population.[305] Policies previously advocated for the development of post-war Europe, heavily influenced by notions of social justice and equality, and should anchor development strategies. Galbraith formulated economic proposals emphasizing food, clothing, shelter, education and medicines for low-income families.[306] The result is special claims for those in need that correspond to economic, social and cultural rights. The selective use of human rights as part of development remains a prevalent threat to the system's legitimacy if it is associated with an economic agenda.

Global Justice and Economic Equality

Article one of the Universal Declaration of Human Rights is based on equality. It states, 'All human beings are born free and equal in dignity and rights.' Yet, many people born in developing states are not equal in these terms. As the citizens of Orwell's *Animal Farm* found economic mismanagement and greed ensured that, 'All animals are equal, but some animals are more equal than others.'[307] International relations discourse ties economic equality to distributive justice. Equality and justice

---

299 See Kothari, S. and Sethi, H. (eds) (1989), *Rethinking Human Rights: Challenges for Theory and Action* (New York: New Horizons Press); Muzaffar, C. (1993), *Human Rights and World Order* (Penang: Just World Trust).

300 Falk, R. (2002), 'Interpreting the Interaction of Global Markets and Human Rights', in Brysk, A. (ed.), *Globalization and Human Rights* (London: University of California Press), 69.

301 'Stand Up For You Rights: The Old Stuffy Ones, That Is: Newer Ones are Distractions', *The Economist* (24 March 2007), 12.

302 Stiglitz, J., *supra* n.148, 20-5.

303 *Ibid.*

304 York, G. (6 Nov 2006), 'China, Africa Forging Closer Ties', *The Globe and Mail*, A10.

305 Sallot, J. (22 Nov 2006), 'Envoy Urges Patience on Rights in China', *The Globe and Mail*, A6.

306 Galbraith, K. (1964), *Economic Development* (Harvard University Press).

307 Orwell, G. (1946), *Animal Farm* (Penguin).

are the basis of the important ethical and political proposals for global governance.[308] This justice implies a set of claims based on equity and equality.[309] Human rights law, and particularly economic, social and cultural rights, represents a similar set of claims tied to the concept of distributive justice. Under human rights law, these claims are universal and impose obligations.

The principles enshrined in articles 22, 25 and 28 of the Universal Declaration of Human Rights, which are the foundation of economic, social and cultural rights and international responsibility, must become central to governance.[310] This implies economic justice and equality at the national and international levels. Economic, social and cultural rights articulate a set of claims that provide a safety net, ensuring a measure of equality and justice at the national level. The Baron de Montesquieu wrote in the mid-eighteenth century: 'all men are born equal, but they do not stay equal. Society takes it from them, and it is only through law that they can become equal again'.[311]

Law, as outlined by Montesquieu in this passage, functions to promote equality, which is distinguished from equal treatment. Equality means economic, social and cultural equality, rather than the formal equality that is the primary feature of most legal systems.[312] The use of unequal treatment to achieve equality as a result necessitates favourable treatment for those who are socially, economically or culturally deprived. It also may imply unfavourable treatment for advantaged citizens. This ideal of affirmative action can be traced throughout human rights treaties.[313]

---

308   See Sen, A. (1992), *Inequality Reexamined* (Harvard University Press); Nozick, R. (1974), *Anarchy, State and Utopia* (New York: Basic Books); Rawls, J., *supra* n.167; Marx, K. (1891), *Critique of the Gotha Programme* (reprint: International Press, 1977).

309   Felice, W., *supra* n.29, 39.

310   Universal Declaration of Human Rights (10 Dec 1948), UNGA res. 217A (III), UN Doc. A/810 at 71 (UDHR). Article 22 reads: 'Everyone, as a member of society, has the right to social security and is entitled to realization, through national effort and international co-operation and in accordance with the organization and resources of each State, of the economic, social and cultural rights indispensable for his dignity and the free development of his personality'. Article 25(1) reads: 'Everyone has the right to a standard of living adequate for the health and well-being of himself and of his family, including food, clothing, housing and medical care and necessary social services, and the right to security in the event of unemployment, sickness, disability, widowhood, old age or other lack of livelihood in circumstances beyond his control'. Article 28 states: 'Everyone is entitled to a social and international order in which the rights and freedoms set forth in this Declaration can be fully realized'.

311   de Secondat Montesquieu, C. (1748), *De l'Esprit des Lois* (reprinted: Paris : Éditions Gallimard, 1995), Livre VIII, Chapître III.

312   Vierdag, E., *supra* n.94, 17-8.

313   E.g. The International Convention on the Elimination of All forms of Racial Discrimination, adopted 21 Dec 1965, entered into force 4 Jan 1969, G.A. Res. 2106 (XX), Annex, 20 U.N. GAOR Supp. (No. 14), at 47, U.N. Doc. A/6014 (1966), 660 U.N.T.S. 195 (ICERD), the first human rights treaty, advocates in its Article 2(2): 'States Parties shall, when the circumstances so warrant, take, in the social, economic, cultural and other fields, special and concrete measures to ensure the adequate development and protection of certain racial groups or individuals belonging to them, for the purpose of guaranteeing them the full

Claims to global distributive justice must be emphasized, given that global economic and social structures reinforce unfair disadvantages and advantages. Global redistribution of resources can help to overcome social injustice internationally and nationally. Social injustice refers to the effect of inequitable political, legal and economic policies governing social institutions.[314] This requires paying attention to public goods and assuring equal access to them. Examples of such goods include nutrition, sanitation, shelter, clothing, education and health care. When a state is unable or unwilling to fulfill obligations surrounding public goods, the international community's obligations must be triggered.

Economic equality is the foundation for the provision of economic, social and cultural rights.[315] The provision of these rights is central to the reduction of poverty and underdevelopment that cause instability and violence.[316] Global failure to fulfill human rights cannot be attributed to national governments alone. The Secretary General of the United Nations has acknowledged:

> ... states, however, cannot do the job alone. We need an active civil society and a dynamic private sector. Both occupy an increasingly large and important share of the space formerly reserved for states alone, and it is plain that the goals outlined here will not be achieved without their full engagement.[317]

When global factors are contributing to global poverty and injustice, then global institutions must be responsible and must take action. It could be possible, provided that:

> ... we accept that all persons involved in upholding social institutions have a shared moral responsibility to ensure that these institutions satisfy at least the universal core criterion of basic justice, which is to ensure that the human rights of all persons affected by these social institutions are fulfilled.[318]

The state should act on behalf of its citizens through international relations.[319] Globalization requires strong institutions capable of ensuring the ability and willingness of states to fulfill this obligation. The United Nations is the only global institution capable of doing so as its mandate encompasses security, development

---

and equal enjoyment of human rights and fundamental freedoms'. On the concept of 'special measures' and redistributive justice in the UN treaties generally, See Marc Bossuyt, Special Rapporteur on Affirmative Action (17 June 2002), Commission on Human Rights, Final Report on 'Prevention of Discrimination. The concept and practice of affirmative action', UN Doc. E/CN.4/Sub.2/2002/21.

314 Felice, W., *supra* n.29, 39.

315 *Ibid.*, 38.

316 'In Larger Freedom: Towards Development, Security, and Human Rights for All', Report of the Secretary-General (2005), UN Doc A/59/2005, para.16.

317 *Ibid.*, para.20.

318 Pogge, T. (1999), 'Human Flourishing and Universal Justice', *Social Philosophy and Policy* 16.1, 358.

319 Goldstein, J., *supra* n.25.

and human rights. This requires an emboldened United Nations that must strengthen states in order to promote human rights.[320]

Acceptance of an international responsibility for global justice does not reduce the responsibility of developing states. Developing states should not participate in institutions that fail to ensure basic justice. But this is not a realistic possibility in the current system.[321] Instead, national and international cooperation is required in order to reform these institutions and/or compensate those adversely affected.

Issues of justice and equality are considered internal problems of developing states to be ameliorated through good governance.[322] The good governance agenda ignores the interdependency of national and international social institutions. Pogge has referred to the stress on national factors as 'explanatory nationalism'.[323] Explanatory nationalism emphasizes that bad domestic policies and institutions have failed to capitalize on the opportunities presented by economic globalization. Some states have taken advantage of the process and become successful while others have floundered. The result is widespread avoidable poverty.[324] Explanatory nationalism conveniently shifts the burden of responsibility away from developed states. This allows the current development programme to remain.

The international context of development failure is crucial in explaining unfulfilled human rights problems and global poverty. Pogge explains that:

> ... global factors significantly influence national policies and institutions, especially in poorer and weaker countries. It is quite possible that, in a different global environment, national factors that tend to generate poverty, or tend to undermine the fulfillment of human rights more generally, would occur much less frequently or not at all.[325]

There is little self-criticism or constructive ideas for improving the global economic system within the dialogue on good governance.[326] It promotes market expansion as synonymous with good governance including democratization, the rule of law and therefore development.[327] This has de-politicized the concepts of democracy and state management and insulates proponents from allegations of undermining state sovereignty.[328] The good governance agenda assumes a leading role for the private sector in development. It takes little account of income distribution inequalities or

---

320   'In Larger Freedom: Towards Development, Security, and Human Rights for All', *supra* n.316, para.21.

321   Pogge, T., *supra* n.318, 359.

322   Uvin, P., *supra* n.261, 4.

323   Pogge, T. (1998), 'The Bounds of Nationalism', *Canadian Journal of Philosophy* 22, 463.

324   Ibid., 463-504

325   Pogge, T., *supra* n.318, 357.

326   Slim, H. (2002), 'Response to Peter Uvin: Making the Moral Low-Ground: Rights as a Struggle for Justice and the Abolition of Development' *Fletcher Journal of Development Studies* 17, 18.

327   *Report of the Secretary-General on globalization and its impact on the full enjoyment of all human rights.* UN Doc: A/58/257 (2003), para.42(c).

328   Uvin, P., *supra* n.261, 4.

the natural environment.[329] This agenda ensures a process of development safe for investors while ignoring the full spectrum of human rights law. It is also patronizing, for the good governance record of the developed states is assumed to be superior.

The possibility that the international community has failed to act collectively or, even worse, deliberately exploited developing states is not considered. Developing states are essential components of the global economy, yet global transactions are not connected with domestic human rights failure.[330] Linking global political economy to the failure of states leads to the uncomfortable question: 'What entitles a small global elite – the affluent citizens of the rich countries – to enforce a global property regime under which they can claim the world's natural resources for themselves and can distribute these amongst themselves on mutually agreeable terms?'[331]

Prioritizing good governance is a valuable strategy for poverty reduction and development. It is a vital component of international development. The Secretary General of the United Nations has explained that development strategy will fail unless 'supported by states with transparent, accountable systems of governance, grounded in the rule of law, encompassing civil and political as well as economic and social rights, and underpinned by accountable and efficient public administration'.[332] However, it cannot replace international responsibility and action. In this context, the Secretary General notes that, ' ... lacking basic infrastructure, human capital and public administration, and burdened by disease, environmental degradation and limited natural resources, these countries cannot afford the basic investments needed to move onto a new path of prosperity unless they receive sustained, targeted external support'.[333]

Not all entrants in the global investment competition are starting from the same point in the competition. It is clear that a system based on justice and equality requires special measures to further the development of developing states. The Report of the Working Group on the Right to Development noted that the equal treatment of unequal parties in the context of development entrenches disparities.[334] The Least Developed Countries report compiled by the United Nations Conference on Trade and Development explained that the poorest and least able segments of the world have been brought into an open global market unprepared, and in a position of weakness.[335]

---

329 UNGA (7 Aug 2003), 'Globalization and its Impact on the Full Enjoyment of All Human Rights', UN Doc. A/58/257, para.45.

330 Pogge, T., *supra* n.318, 359.

331 *Ibid.*, 360.

332 'In Larger Freedom: Towards Development, Security, and Human Rights for All', *supra* n.316, para.36.

333 *Ibid.*, para.33.

334 'The Right to Development', Report of the Working Group on the Right to Development on its 5th session, 14-18 Nov 2005, UN Doc. E/CN.4/2004/23/Add.1, para.18(w).

335 United Nations Conference on Trade and Development (UNCTAD) (2000), *The Least Developed Countries 2000 Report, Aid, Private Capital Flows and External Debt: The Challenge of Financing Development in the LDCs* (Geneva: UNCTAD), 25.

It is essential for human rights to be upheld in relation to globalization for the purpose of global justice. Dominant actors may prefer a reduced concept of human rights, limited to a constitutional electoral process and protection of the individual from government.[336] In order to avoid this, economic globalization must be regulated to become inclusive, participatory and accountable to the world's people.[337]

Conclusion

The fulfillment of human rights by States is problematic within the context of globalization. Despite this, states remain at the heart of international relations and should remain central to human rights responsibility. Economic globalization based on foreign investment is the engine of growth accepted nearly universally by states as the only model for development. The human rights project, set out in the Charter of the United Nations and the Bill of Rights, lags far behind in implementation and realization. The unwillingness of governments to regulate in terms of public policy due to economic considerations is apparent. States have begun to sacrifice regulatory ability in an irreversible manner. States must be able to direct their own developmental priorities through experimentation and the development of regulatory frameworks.[338] The role of the state is crucial in mitigating inequality and social justice issues as well as environmental degradation.[339]

Bilateral investment agreements are independent from each other but form an interwoven network.[340] This network is becoming a *de facto* development system. However, it suffers from a democratic deficit in its governance, formulation and interpretation. The perception of economic globalization as exploitative may render it unsustainable. The investment-based development system is perceived as unaccountable to human rights law. Yet, these same agreements form a fundamental aspect of global governance, and the parties to them are subjects of international law.

The global investment project, in order to quell discontent, needs to operate democratically by ensuring the ability of states to fulfill human rights law. The promotion of rights-based development leads to questions of implementation and justiciability.[341] The answers to these questions are crucial to the notion of accountability, participation and empowerment of the peoples of the developing

---

336   Ignatieff, M. (1999), *Whose Universal Values? The Crisis in Human Rights* (The Hague: Praemium Erasmianum Foundation), 43-54.

337   Falk, R., *supra* n.300, 69

338   Moran, T. (2001), *Parental Supervision: The New Paradigm for FDI and Development.* (Washington, D.C.: Institute for International Economics).

339   Stiglitz, J., *supra* n.110, xiii.

340   Schneiderman, D., *supra* n.100, 766.

341   Arbour, L. (2006), 'Using Human Rights to Reduce Poverty', in *Development Outreach* (World Bank Institute); *Paschim Banga Khet Mazdoor Samity v State of West Bengal* [1996], SOL Case No. 169, 4 SCC 25, 3 SCJ 25, 2 CHRLD 109; *PUCL v. Union of India and Others*, Writ Petition [Civil] 196 of 2001; *Government of the Republic of South Africa and Others v Grootboom*, 2001 [1] SA 46 [CC], 2000 [11] BCLR 1169 [CC]; *Viceconte, Mariela*

world.[342] Here the focus remains on the international obligation to ensure an environment in which states are willing to implement promote, protect and fulfill these rights rather than on technical details that require an in-depth study of their own.

The burgeoning international investment protection regime contributes to the marginalization of large sections of the world's population. These marginalized people perceive the regime as an instrument of domination of rich over poor, north over south and investment interests over human rights.[343] A rift is evident on these issues between the developed and developing states of the international community. The right to development addresses the fact that developing states need assistance. This requires strategic domestic planning through public regulation, which is precisely the governmental facet being sacrificed to the investment project. The right to development requires states to ensure human rights are advanced by development and calls for international responsibility for the creation of an international system that addresses equality and justice. The discourse on the right to development addresses many of the concerns outlined in this chapter and will now be developed in greater detail.

---

v. Estado Nacional – Ministerio de Salud y Ministerio de Economía de la Nación [1998]; *International Commission of Jurists v Portugal*, Complaint No. 1/1998.

342   See Craven, M. (1998), *The International Covenant on Economic, Social, and Cultural Rights: A Perspective on Its Development* (Oxford University Press); Eide, A. et al. (eds) (2001), *Economic, Social and Cultural rights: A Textbook* (Dordrecht: Martinus Nijhoff Publishers; Scott, C. and Macklem, J. (1992), 'Constitutional Ropes of Sand or Justiciable Guarantees? Social Rights in a New South African Constitution', *University of Pennsylvania Law Review* 141.

343   Shalankany, A., *supra* n.76, 423.

Chapter 3

Development Cooperation in Theory: The Right to Development

Introduction

The right to development outlines a rights-based process which can help to reduce the problems of globalization. It provides a solid foundation for development from which human rights can be realized. The right to development articulates the entitlement of the developing world.[1] The international community has confirmed it as an inalienable and universal human right.[2] The right to development remains unimplemented and is overshadowed by globalization.

The recognition of the right to development should advance the concept of development beyond economic growth. Article 1 of The Declaration on the Right to Development states that: 'The right to development is an inalienable human right by virtue of which every human person and all peoples are entitled to participate in, contribute to, and enjoy economic, social, cultural and political development, in which all human rights and fundamental freedoms can be fully realized.'[3] The right to development is considered a right to a process that affords human rights entitlements.[4]

The right to development entails obligations at both the national and international levels that are increasingly applicable in a globalized world. The United Nations High Commissioner for Human Rights in her statement to the Working Group on the Right to Development clarified that the right to development is an obligation of states that must be ensured at the national level. Contemporaneously, she emphasized that this entails collective responsibility towards the creation of an enabling environment for national implementation. The High Commissioner called attention to the fact that the Declaration on the Right to Development provides the international community with, 'a powerful manifestation that every human person and all peoples are entitled to participate in, contribute to, and enjoy economic, social, cultural and political

---

1   Lindroos, A (1999), *The Right to Development* (University of Helsinki), 29.
2   Vienna Declaration and Programme for Action, World Conference on Human Rights, Vienna, 14–25 June 1993, UN Doc. A/CONF.157/24 (Part I) at 20 (Vienna Declaration and Programme for Action), Part 1, para.10.
3   Declaration on the Right to Development (4 Dec 1986), UNGA Res. 41/128, annex 41, Supp. No. 53 at 186, UN Doc. A/41/53 (DRD).
4   Amede Obiora, L. (1996), 'Beyond the Rhetoric of a Right to Development', *Law and Policy* 18, 389.

development, in which all human rights and fundamental freedoms can be realized'.[5] Accordingly, the international community should support domestic policies that favour rights-based development.[6]

The Declaration advocates self-determination, full national sovereignty over resources and the preservation of the ability of the state in question to formulate rights-based policy.[7] The right to development is a commitment to Article 28 of the Universal Declaration of Human Rights, which provides that, 'Everyone is entitled to a social and international order in which the rights and freedoms set forth in this Declaration can be fully realized.'[8] The Declaration on the Right to Development does not provide absolute instructions for states but provides a framework required to realize the right. It addresses the important notion of agency, defining development as a human right with people as its subjects. It clarifies that states acting at the national and international levels are the duty-bearers.

This framework provides a basis for defining the right to development, which has become a legitimate source of law pertaining to development and thereby globalization.[9] While it does not create new rights, it defines a process of duties to be integrated into globalization.[10] Obligations associated with the right to development that address international cooperation are in the process of crystallization and require clarification.[11] Nevertheless, in a global world where state-centric obligations have become blurred, the right to development provides guidance by asserting global responsibilities.

The right to development should provide an ethical framework for globalization.[12] The individual is the rights-holder and the state is the duty-bearer and instrument of obtaining rights *vis-à-vis* the international community. The Declaration emphasizes that the state remains responsible for ensuring rights domestically.[13] However, it calls for collective action by states to address global problems.[14] This does not distract from the state's primary national duty, but stresses the crucial element of

5   Statement by Louise Arbour, UN High Commissioner for Human Rights to the Working Group on the Right to Development (Geneva, 15 February 2005, Palais des Nations Room XVII) (available online <www.unhchr.ch/huricane/huricane.nsf/view01/4D3A47B9D07F2348C1256FA900575AEF?opendocument>, accessed 15 March 2008).

6   DRD, Articles 2(3), 3(3) and 8.

7   *Ibid.*, Articles 1 and 2.

8   Universal Declaration of Human Rights (10 Dec 1948), UNGA Res 217A (III), UN Doc. A/810 at 71 (UDHR), Article 28.

9   Matua, M. (1996), 'Editor's Introduction', *Law and Policy* 18, 195; Orford, A. (2002), 'Globalization and the Right to Development', in Alston, P. (ed.) (2002), *Peoples' Rights* (Oxford University Press), 135.

10   Sengupta, A. (2002), 'On the Theory and Practice of the Right to Development', *Human Rights Quarterly* 24.4, 846.

11   Donnelly, J. (1985), 'In Search of the Unicorn: The Jurisprudence and Politics of the Right to Development', *California Western International Law Journal* 15, 473.

12   Report of the open-ended Working Group on the Right to Development on its 3rd session, UN Doc. E/CN.4/2002/28/Rev.1., para.38.

13   DRD, Articles 2(3), 3(1) and 8.

14   *Ibid.*, Articles 3(3), 4, 5, 6, 7, and 10.

international cooperation.[15] The right to development is therefore directly relevant to globalization as it puts forward corresponding global responsibilities.

International cooperation is possible despite the national interest priorities of realist international relations. States have successfully cooperated in areas of convergent economic interests but not on the right to development. Cooperation often breaks down over international resource distribution. Developed states have in the past rejected legal obligations to cooperate internationally to fulfill the right to development while developing states have steadfastly supported it.[16] Developed states have narrowly defined international cooperation in a manner that inadequately addresses accountability in a global economy. As a result, the obligations set forth in by the right to development have not been elaborated on with authority.[17] The refusal to recognize cooperative legal obligations has prevented the legal development of the right.

Developed states make rhetorical promises concerning human rights. Yet, when economic interests are at stake, states prioritize national interests by abstaining or voting against binding rules.[18] As a result, despite near universal acceptance on paper the right to development has not been realized in practice for the majority of people.[19] The United Nations High Commissioner for Human Rights has lamented that the failure to make binding commitments towards the fulfillment of the right to development has discredited efforts at global governance.[20] The international community has instead focused cooperation on promoting globalization that may circumvent human rights.[21]

The right to development's effectiveness suffers from political and economic constraints that affect its implementation and interpretation but The Declaration is a source of law. In practice, the most valuable provisions of the Declaration on the Right to Development have been misconstrued while its human rights

---

15   Gross Espiell, H. (1991), 'Introduction: Community-oriented rights', in Bedjaoui, M. (ed.), *International Law: Achievements and Prospects* (Dordrecht: Martinus Nijhoff), 1170.

16   See Lennox, M. and Salomon, C. (2003), 'Negotiating the Right to Development for Minorities', *McGill International Review* 4.1.

17   *Ibid.*

18   Marks, S. (2004), 'The Human Right to Development: Between Rhetoric and Reality', *Harvard Human Rights Law Journal* 17, 137.

19   Report of the Working Group on the Right to Development on its 5th session, UN Doc. E/CN.4/2004/23/ADD.1 (2004).

20   Statement by Louise Arbour, *supra* n.5.

21   See Canova, T. (2000), 'Financial Liberalization, International Monetary Disorder, and the Neoliberal State', *American University International Law Review* 15, 1280; Shelton, D. (2002), 'Symposium: Globalization and the Erosion of Sovereignty in Honour of Professor Lichtenstein: Protecting Human Rights in a Globalized World' *Boston College International and Comparative Law Revue* 25, 273; Morgan-Foster, J. (2003), 'The Relationship of the IMF Structural Adjustment programmes to Economic, Social and Cultural Rights: The Argentine Case Revisited', *Michigan Journal of International Law* 24, 577; Stiglitz, J. (2003), *Globalization and its Discontents* (Norton); Marks, S., *supra* n.18; Sengupta, A., Fifth Report of the Independent Expert on the Right to Development, Submitted in Accordance with Commission on Human Rights, Resolution 2002/69, UN Doc. E/CN.4/2002/wg.18/6., para.5 and 6.

language has often been ignored.[22] While it retains the status of a declaration and not a treaty, the Declaration on the Right to Development has important political and legal ramifications. The international community overwhelmingly supports it and refers to it in most development goals and policy.[23] Its political and moral importance is no longer in question. Yet the right to development, in order to have discernable legal content, must meet formal criteria. The right's content must be clarified.

The debate surrounding the right to development cannot be understood through legal analysis alone. The amalgamated interchange of international relations, international law, political and economic interests, economic growth and the advancement of human rights all combine to form the context of development. This is why the right to development is so valuable. The negative aspects of global investment affecting development and human rights transcend national and academic boundaries and are influenced by non-state actors. Human rights law must address this shift.

The Importance of the Right to Development

The Declaration on the Right to Development contributes positively to the development discourse in three ways. First, it addresses the link between economic globalization, development and human rights law in terms of international obligations. Second, it reasserts the interdependence and universality of all human rights as part of the development process. Finally, it establishes a rights-based framework for the development process that can guide state action.

The duty of states to cooperate to achieve the objectives of the Charter of the United Nations is essential for development.[24] The preamble of the Declaration on the Right to Development links these international development obligations to those contained in Article 28 of the Universal Declaration of Human Rights by noting that, 'under the provisions of the Universal Declaration of Human Rights everyone is entitled to a social and international order in which the rights and freedoms set forth in that Declaration can be fully realized'.[25] It clearly promotes accountability through international cooperation. The Working Group on the Right to Development in its 2002 Report emphasized that, 'The distinguishing element of the right to development, therefore, is an enabling international environment and a just and equitable international system that is favourable to development. Greater attention needs to be given to this element of the right to development.'[26]

---

22   Uvin, P. (2002), 'On Moral High Ground: The Incorporation of Human Rights by the Development Enterprise', *PRAXIS: The Fletcher Journal of Development Studies* 27, 4.

23   Orford, A., *supra* n.9, 171.

24   The Charter of the United Nations (adopted 26 June 1945, entered into force 24 Oct 1945), 59 Stat. 1031, T.S. 993, 3 Bevans 1153.

25   DRD, Preamble.

26   Report of the open-ended Working Group on the Right to Development on its 3rd session, *supra* n.12, para.52.

The Declaration on the Right to Development emphasizes the interdependence of all human rights previously divided by the politics of the Cold War. Interdependence was addressed in the Declaration on the Right to Development that was adopted because the General Assembly was:

> ... concerned at the existence of serious obstacles to development, as well as to the complete fulfillment of human beings and of peoples, constituted, *inter alia*, by the denial of civil, political, economic, social and cultural rights, and considering that all human rights and fundamental freedoms are indivisible and interdependent and that, in order to promote development, equal attention and urgent consideration should be given to the implementation, promotion and protection of civil, political, economic, social and cultural rights and that, accordingly, the promotion of, respect for and enjoyment of certain human rights and fundamental freedoms cannot justify the denial of other human rights and fundamental freedoms.[27]

The Declaration proclaims that, 'All human rights and fundamental freedoms are indivisible and interdependent; equal attention and urgent consideration should be given to the implementation, promotion and protection of civil, political, economic, social and cultural rights', and that, 'states should take steps to eliminate obstacles to development resulting from failure to observe civil and political rights, as well as economic social and cultural rights'.[28]

A rights-based approach is implicit in a number of articles found in the right to development.[29] The rights-based approach uses the language and legal tools of human rights law to promote participation, non-discrimination, empowerment and accountability as necessary benchmarks for development initiatives.[30] It is considered the cornerstone of the right to development and essential for its practical realization.[31] The rights-based approach can help ensure that national policy makes foreign investment beneficial to development.[32] The Commission on Human Rights explains that, 'The right to development involves more than development itself; it implies a human rights approach to development, which is something new.'[33] Marks explains the relationship between the rights-based approach and the right to development as follows:

> The human rights-based approach to development should be applied as part of the right to development, but it may also involve isolating a particular issue, such as health, and

---

27 DRD, Preamble.

28 *Ibid.* Articles 6(1) and 6(2).

29 *Ibid.* Articles 1, 2, 3, 6, 8, and 10.

30 Report of United Nations Development Programme to the 61st Session of the UN Commission on Human Rights, UN Doc. E/CN.4/2005/133, paras.24 and 28; Van Weerelt, P. (2001), *A Human-Rights-Approach to Development Programming in the UNDP: Adding a Missing Link* (UNDP), 1.

31 Report of the open-ended Working Group on the Right to Development on its 3rd session, *supra* n.12, paras.12 and 57.

32 *Ibid.*, para.38.

33 Report of the Working Group on the Right to Development, UN Doc. E/CN.4/1995/11, para.44.

applying to that issue a clear understanding of the state's obligations under the relevant international human rights instruments and the insights applicable to project implementation derived from authorized interpretations of those obligations, such as General Comment 14 adopted by the Committee on Economic, Social and Cultural Rights on the right to health. Thus, the right to development implies both a critical review of the development process in a given country and a program of action to integrate a human rights approach within all aspects of that process.[34]

Two other important concepts are addressed in the Declaration on the Right to Development. These are the, 'equality of opportunity in access to basic resources', and 'fair distribution of income', both of which may be conditions for the exercise of democratic rights.[35] There is a duty on all states to democratize national institutions. The Declaration on the Right to Development insists on 'active, free and meaningful participation'.[36] The participatory rights restated in the Declaration are evident in a number of United Nations human rights instruments[37] as well as in the Charter of Economic Rights and Duties of States[38] and the prominent development strategies of the international community developed at international conferences on the subject since the 1970s.[39]

The right to development has ascended from controversial beginnings as a statement of developed world goals to a prominent legal aspect of the international community's development policy. The right has become a secure part of the legal framework of international human rights law.[40] This goes a long way towards establishing the legitimacy of the right to development within the international community.

---

34   Marks, S. (2001), *The Human Rights Framework for Development: Five Approaches* (Working Paper No. 6, Francois-Xavier Bagnoud Center for Health and Human Rights, Harvard School of Public Health), 11.

35   DRD, Articles 1(1) (defining development), 8(1) and 8(2) (participation as a factor in development).

36   *Ibid.* Article 2(3).

37   International Covenant on Civil and Political Rights (adopted 16 Dec 1966, entered into force 23 Mar 1976), G.A. Res. 2200A (XXI), 21 UN GAOR Supp. No. 16 at 52, UN Doc. A/6316 (1966), 999 UNT.S. 171 (ICCPR), Article 25; Declaration on Social Progress and Development, G.A. Res. 2542 (XXIV), 24 UN GAOR Supp. (No. 30) at 49, UN Doc. A/7630 (1969), Articles 5 and 15; see also: Ganji, M. (1975), *The Realization of Economic Social, and Cultural Rights: Problems, Policies, Progress*, UN Doc. E/CN.4/1108/rev.1 (New York: UN), Ch. 11; Ferrero, R. (1983), *Study of the New International Economic Order and the Promotion of Human Rights*, UN Doc. E/CN.4/Sub.2/1983/24, Adds. 1 and 2 (New York: UN), paras.152 and 288; Study by the Secretary-General on Popular Participation (1985), UN Doc. E/CN.4/1985/10.

38   Charter of Economic Rights and Duties of States (1 May 1974), G.A. Res. 3281 (XXIX), UN GAOR, 29th Sess., Supp. No. 31 (1974).

39   Declaration of Principles and Programme of Action of the World Employment Conference(1976), UN Doc. E/5857, Article 3; Report of the World Conference on Agrarian Reform and Rural Development (1979), UN Doc. A/54/485 at 8; Vienna Declaration and Programme of Action; A/CONF.157/23(12 July 1993; United Nations Millennium Declaration (8 Sept 2000), G.A. Res. 55/2, UN GAOR, 55th Sess., Supp. No. 49, at 4, UN Doc. A/55/49.

40   Orford, A., *supra* n.9, 135.

However, the right to development's status as human rights law does not ensure its implementation, as implementation remains subject to political will. Global development strategies are dominated by the Millennium Development Goals, which like the Declaration on the Right to Development is also expressed in a General Assembly resolution, and by the Poverty Reduction Strategies promoted by the international financial institutions. These influence the debate on international development, and domestic and donor development policies much more than the human rights law concept of the right to development. From a human rights perspective, the right to development should be more important for its rights-based approach. However, legal scholars should be wary of overestimating its current importance in a global system based on self interest.

The right to development requires states to coordinate development for the benefit of individuals.[41] Clearly, this rights-based process, linked explicitly to interdependent human rights law and thus entailing international obligations on States, has far reaching political and economic connotations. One of the obstacles to the achievement of the right to development is inequality in international relations.[42] Thus, a political and economic examination is beneficial in identifying the contextual development of this right.

Development of the Right to Development

The slow development of the right to development is due to its highly politicized nature. Indeed, it holds a revolutionary character in terms of global economics, requiring justice and equality to trump market-based decision making. It was postulated in the 1970s as new set of initiatives emerged directly challenging the economics of the international community.[43]

Human rights law has continually evolved.[44] Alston has given such dynamism impetus by declaring this evolution, 'the essential energy of the tradition of human rights'.[45] Decolonization revolutionized international society and the forces unleashed took aim at international law. The bourgeois and socialist revolutions had given rise to first and second-generation civil and political, then social, economic and cultural

---

41   DRD, Article 2(1).

42   United Nation Commission on Human Rights (26 Sept 1990), Report on the Global Consultation on the Realization of the Right to Development as a Human Right, UN Doc. E/CN.4/ 1990/9/Rev.1, Chapter 7, para.147.

43   See General Assembly Resolution (12 Nov 1984), The Rights of People to Peace, UN Doc. G.A. Res. 39/11; Alston, P. (ed.), *supra* n.9.

44   Vasak, K. (1990), 'Les Differentes Categories des Droits de l'Homme', in Lapeyre, A., de Tinguy, F. and Vasak, K. (eds), *Les Dimensions Universelles des Droits de l'Homme* (Bruxelles: Bruylant), 297.

45   Alston, P. (1982), 'A Third Generation of Solidarity Rights: Progressive Development or Obfuscation of International Human Rights Law?' *Netherlands International Law Review* 33, 314.

rights. The anti-colonial movement gave rise to third generation solidarity rights, including the right to development.[46]

The numerically dominant group of newly independent states,[47] brought economic development issues to the agenda of the international community.[48] These states, having gained political independence, were eager to assert their economic independence as well.[49] They became frustrated at the exploitative global economy.[50] This movement called for a new international economic order,[51] which culminated with the Declaration on the Establishment of a New International Economic Order and the Charter of Rights and Duties of states, adopted by the General Assembly in 1974 and 1975.[52] Attempts at reform of the international economic institutions proved unsuccessful.[53]

The Senegalese jurist M'Baye posited the right to development[54] as part of Vasek's third generation of rights.[55] The third generation rights are rights of solidarity amongst the international community to ensure a system conducive to human rights.[56] These solidarity rights, while controversial as is apparent from the refusal of developed states to recognize them, directly address the problem of common goods relevant

---

46   Marks, S. (1981), 'Emerging Human Rights: A New Generation for the 1980s?' *Rutgers Law Review* 33, 440; G.A. Res. 1161 (XII), UN GAOR, 3rd Comm., 12th Sess., Agenda Item 12, UN Doc. A/3716 (1957), para.12(3); Proclamation of the International Conference on Human Rights, UN GAOR, at 4., UN Doc. A/CONF.32/41 (1968), paras.12 and 13.

47   See Declaration on the Granting of Independence to Colonial Countries and Peoples, 14 Dec 1960, G.A. Res. 1514 (XV); Implementation of the Declaration on the Granting of Independence to Colonial Countries and Peoples, Report of the Special Political and Decolonization Committee, UN GAOR 4th Comm., 54th Sess. at 5, UN Doc. A/54/584 (1999).

48   Alston, P. (1991), 'Revitalizing United Nations Work on the Right to Development', *Melbourne University Law Review* 18, 218 .

49   Bedjaoui, M. (1991), 'The Right to Development', in Bedjaoui, M. (ed.), *supra* n.15, 1177.

50   Raghavan, C. (1990), *Recolonization: GATT, The Uruguay Round and the Third World* (Penang, Malaysia: Third World Network), 51.

51   Rosas, A. (1995), 'The Right to Development', in Eide, A. et al. (eds), *Economic, Social and Cultural Rights: A Text Book* (Dordrecht: Martinus Nijhoff), 247.

52   Declaration on the Establishment of a New Economic Order, adopted 1 May 1974, G.A. Res. 3201 (S-VI), 6 (SPECIAL) UN GAOR, 6th Spec. Sess. Supp. No. 1, at 3, UN Doc. A/9559 (1974); Charter of Economic Rights and Duties of States.

53   Raghavan, C., *supra* n.50, 52.

54   M'Baye, K. (1972), 'Le Droit au Développement comme un Droit de l'Homme', *Revue des Droits de l'Homme* 5.2-3, 505-534.

55   Vasak, K. (1977), 'A 30 Year Struggle: The Sustained Effort to Give Force to the Law of the Universal Declaration of Human Rights', *UNESCO Courier*; Vasak, K. (1984), 'Pour une Troisieme generation des Droits de l'Homme', in Swinarski, C. (ed.), *Studies and Essays on International Humanitarian Law and Red Cross Principles* (Geneva: Martinus Nijhoff); Vasak, K., *supra* n.44, 301-09; see also Marks, S., *supra* n.46, 435.

56   Gross Espiell, H., *supra* n.15, 1167.

in globalization.[57] While all human rights require solidarity in some form, this third generation requires a greater degree of international cooperation.[58]

The developed states of the international community and its pre-existing economic institutions steadfastly ignored these calls for change in practice.[59] The initiatives were successfully opposed by developed industrial powers, who blamed corrupt regimes and poor governance for poverty in the developing world.[60] This division occurred due to the enormous political and economic consequences involved in restructuring the international economic system. The developed states and underdeveloped states took up ideologically opposed positions on the viability of this revolutionary action.[61] The developed states turned to conditionality put forward by the international financial institutions to ensure their own interests.[62]

As the efforts to formulate the New International Economic Order faded, developing states grasped the right to development as a legal mechanism to promote their political and economic goals.[63] They believed that economic exploitation is a violation of human rights and that international cooperation for development is a legal obligation, not a charitable one.[64] The developing states staunchly put forth what Abi-Saab described as, 'this bundle of policy measures'.[65] According to Abi Saab, a legally sanctioned right to development must proceed from a new international economic order, which is, 'the only blue-print of the right to development which stands a realistic chance of hardening into law'.[66] Without a just international economic order, the right to development will always succumb to market-based interests.

The United Nations has consistently proceeded on the premise that a right to development exists. The Right to Development was recognized in these terms by the United Nations Commission on Human Rights in 1977.[67] Since then, the United Nations has explored the meanings and implications of this right. Early activities included two seminars of note: The Seminar on the Effects of the Existing Unjust International Economic Order on the Economies of the Developing Countries and the Obstacles That This Represents for the Implementation of Human Rights and Fundamental Freedoms,

---

57   Marks, S., *supra* n.46, 441.
58   Gross Espiell, H., *supra* n.15, 1169.
59   Raghavan, C., *supra* n.50, 54.
60   Barsh, L. (1991), 'The Right to Development as a Human Right: Results of the Global Consultation', *Human Rights Quarterly* 13, 328.
61   Orford, A., *supra* n.9, 130.
62   Raghavan, C., *supra* n.50, 54-58.
63   Lindroos, A., *supra* n.1, 3.
64   Alston, P., *supra* n.48, 218-19.
65   Abi-Saab, G. (1980), 'The Legal Formulation of a Right to Development', in Dupuy, R.-J. (ed.), *The Right to Development at the International Level* (Hague Academy of International Law Workshop), 167.
66   *Ibid.*
67   Commission on Human Rights, 21 Feb 1977, Resolution 4 (XXXIII).

held in Geneva in 1980[68] and the Seminar on the Relations that Exist Between Human Rights, Peace and Development, held in New York in 1981.[69]

At the first of these seminars, 26 of the invited 36 states attended. Also in attendance were three inter-governmental organizations, 19 non-governmental organizations and two national liberation movements. Absentees of note included Japan, the United Kingdom, the United States and West Germany who refused the invitation. This absence was attributed to the controversial nature of the title, which seemed to prejudge the issues on the agenda. Others qualified this absence as an attempt to evade responsibility by powerful industrialized states.[70]

The fifth through ninth meetings of the seminar analyzed the right to development as a human right. Broad agreement was reached that the right did exist and that it was a right of individuals to be implemented by states cooperatively, building upon commitments entailed in the United Nations Charter, the Bill of Rights and the movement towards a New International Economic Order. Other delegates asserted that the right to development was a continuation of third generation rights, or solidarity rights, that included environmental well being, peace, and a new international economic order.[71] Delegates confirmed the need to move forward on international action towards the realization of the right to development. Many delegates called for a binding convention on the right to development.[72]

The Seminar on the Relations that Exist Between Human Rights, Peace and Development, held in New York in 1981 enjoyed the attendance of 28 of 37 invited states including the United States.[73] The less controversial title gave rise to debate on the reality and implications of the right to development.[74] Wide ranging debate reflected differing viewpoints on implementation. Tentative agreement that practical measures and concrete efforts should now be taken seemed evident.[75] This reflected a recent session of the United Nation's Commission on Human Rights which confirmed that conditions already existed for a United Nations Declaration on the

---

68   Seminar on the Effects of the Existing Unjust International Economic Order on the Economies of the Developing Countries and the Obstacles that This Represents for the Implementation of Human Rights and Fundamental Freedoms, 30 June-11 July 1980, Geneva, UN Doc. ST/HR/SER.A/10.

69   Seminar on the Relations that Exist Between Human Rights, Peace and Development, 3-14 August 1981, UN Headquarters, New York, UN Doc. E/1979/36, Supp. No. 6.

70   Glen Mower, A. (1985), *International Cooperation for Social Justice: Global and Regional Protection of Economic/Social Rights* (Westport, CT: Greenwood, 1985), 176.

71   Seminar on the Effects of the Existing Unjust International Economic Order, *supra* n.68.

72   *Ibid.*; see also Glen Mower, A., *supra* n.70, 155.

73   Seminar on the Relations that Exist Between Human Rights, Peace and Development, *supra* n.69, Supp. No.6.5.

74   Glen Mower, A., *supra* n.70, 156.

75   Seminar on the Relations that Exist Between Human Rights, Peace and Development, *supra* n.69, Supp. No. 6.19.

Right to Development.[76] The threat of the communist alternative for developing states may have persuaded Western states to adopt a more conciliatory stance.

As a result of these seminars, the right to development was put forward as a blueprint for globally achieving human rights. In May 1981, the United Nations Economic and Social Council approved the Commission on Human Right's Decision to establish a working group, 'to study the scope and contents of the right to development and the most effective means to ensure the realization in all countries of the economic, social and cultural rights enshrined in the various international instruments'.[77] The agenda of this working group also included producing, 'concrete proposals for the implementation of the right to development and for a draft international instrument on the subject'.[78] The Working Group proposed a Declaration on the subject, but did not rule out the possibility of developing a more binding instrument in the future.

The original draft Declaration emphasized both national and international obligations for implementation.[79] The results were submitted as a progress report outlining the Draft Declaration.[80] The preamble referred to the international obligations entailed in primary texts such as the Charter of the United Nations and the International Bill of Rights. It also insisted on the interdependence of all human rights and the links between peace and development. The draft preamble addressed the roles of the individual, group and state in the implementation of the right to development. The draft reiterates that implementation necessitates reform of the international economic system. Although many differing views remained within the working group, the Chairman felt confident that results would be productive and decisive based on the many areas of agreement.[81]

Significantly, the right to development was enshrined at the time in a legally binding document: The African Charter on Human and Peoples' Rights.[82] The African Charter on Human and Peoples' Rights has combined an impressive array of individual rights and duties, group rights as well as state duties. It recognizes the interdependence of all human rights and includes the right to development, among other solidarity rights.[83] The African Charter states in its article 22:

---

76   Seminar on the Relations that Exist Between Human Rights, Peace and Development, *supra* n.69, Supp. No. 6.20.

77   Commission on Human Rights, 11 March 1981, Resolution 36 (XXXVII).

78   Report of the Working Group of Governmental Experts on the Right to Development, UN Doc. E/CN.4/1489 (1982).

79   Report on the Work of the 4th Session, UN Doc. E/CN.4/AC.39/1982/11.

80   Reports of the Working Group of Governmental Experts on the Right to Development, UN Doc. E/CN.4/1983/11 (1982).

81   Progress Report, UN Doc. E/CN.4/1983, paras.17, 18, 20 and 31.

82   African [Banjul] Charter on Human and Peoples' Rights (adopted 27 June 1981, entered into force 21 Oct 1986), OAU Doc. CAB/LEG/67/3 rev. 5, 21 I.L.M. 58 (1982).

83   *Ibid.*

1. All peoples shall have the right to their economic, social and cultural development with due regard to their freedom and identity and in the equal enjoyment of the common heritage of mankind.
2. States shall have the duty, individually or collectively, to ensure the exercise of the right to development.

Including the right to development confronted the hierarchy of human rights and provided momentum to the right to development's legal evolution.[84] Since Africa is comprised of formerly colonized developing states, the codification of the right to development in this context is particularly relevant.[85] Although the enumeration of rights and duties in international agreements may not achieve the intended ends, 'it serves to give them publicity and entrench them in the minds of men'.[86] The existence of the right to development was no longer in question. As early as 1981, Alston noted that:

> In terms of international human rights law, the existence of the right to development is a fait accompli. Whatever reservations different groups may have as to its legitimacy, viability or usefulness, such doubts are now better left behind and replaced by efforts to ensure that the formal process of elaborating the content of the right is a productive and constructive exercise.[87]

The right finally enshrined in 1986 in the Declaration on the Right to Development.[88] The Declaration elaborates on the content and obligations of the right to development. The vision of the international economic order put forward by the right to development confronted the status quo. It subjected the international legal order to democratic control in favour of the majority that are developing states. The most industrialized states therefore rejected the implantation of the right to development.[89] The developed world insisted that the right to development should not rejuvenate the New International Economic Order.[90] Developing states, by contrast, recognized the failure of 50 years of decolonization and development strategies. They insisted that the

---

84   Heyns, K. (2002), 'Civil and Political Rights in the African Charter', in Evans, M. and Murray, R. (eds), *The African Charter on Human and Peoples' Rights: The System in Practice, 1986-2000* (Cambridge University Press), 137.

85   See Ankumah, E. (1996), *The African Commission on Human and Peoples' Rights* (The Hague: Kluwer Law International); Oji Umozurike, U. (1997), *The African Charter on Human and Peoples' Rights* (The Hague: Martinus Nijhoff); Matua, M. (1999), 'The African Human Rights Court: A Two Legged Stool?' *Human Rights Quarterly* 21, 342.

86   Oji Umozurike, U. (1983), 'Current Development: The African Charter of Human and Peoples Rights', *American Journal of International Law* 77, 911.

87   Alston, P. (1981), 'Development and the Rule of Law: Prevention Versus Cure as a Human Rights Strategy', Working Paper in Development, Human Rights and the Rule of Law: Report of the Conference held in The Hague on 27 April-1 May 1981, printed in *International Review of the International Commission* 26, 106.

88   DRD.

89   Bedjaoui, M. (1991), 'General Introduction', in Bedjaoui, M., *supra* n.15, 98-101.

90   Marks, S., *supra* n.18, 143.

global economic order excluded them from its benefits.[91] Despite resistance from the developed world, the drive for a new international economic order greatly influenced the Declaration on the Right to Development. Indeed, United Nations documents on the right to development and the Declaration on the Right to Development explicitly mention the new international economic order.[92] The Declaration on the Right to Development represented an attempt to address these concerns in an acceptable legal fashion.

Political wrangling often takes precedence over constructive dialogue on the right to development. By drawing attention to the inequalities in international relations, the right has emboldened the developing world, garnering cautious support from Europe and opposition from the United States.[93] The politicization of the right to development was entrenched when the United States cast the lone dissenting vote against the Declaration on the Right to Development, thereby affirming its stance against the political goals of the developing states.[94] Significantly, this influential resistance has prevented the advancement of the right to development both in terms of implementation and as a source of binding legal obligations.[95]

The politics of the right to development have therefore been troublesome. Capital-exporting developed states perceive the right as a threat to foreign investment and thereby globalization in general. Developed states have resisted it in order to ensure that the profitable activities of their corporations and investors are not constrained in the developing world.[96] The General Assembly has noted that capital-exporting states have striven to protect the current apparatus of global investment from this risk.[97] Developed states remain adamant that vital economic matters such as global trade and investment, financial and lending policy and the operations of multinational corporations do not fall under the ambit of the United Nations human rights organs.[98] Development initiatives and the governance of economic globalization in general, should remain based on economic principles. Development, from this point of view, only occurs through private enterprise and market liberalization.[99] The staunch

---

91 Road Map towards the Implementation of the United Nations Millennium Declaration. UNGA 56th Sess., UN Doc. A/56/326 (2001).

92 See Report of the Secretary-General on the International Dimensions of the Right to Development as a Human Right, UN ESCOR, 35th Sess., paras.152-59, UN Doc. E/CN.4/1334 (1979); Report of the Open-Ended Working Group of Governmental Experts on the Right to Development, UN ESCOR, 45th Sess., UN Doc. E/CN.4/1989/10, para.25.

93 See Marks, S., *supra* n.18, 141.

94 *Ibid.*, 140.

95 *Ibid.*

96 Orford, A., *supra* n.9, 133.

97 Press Release, UN GAOR, 57th Sess., 57th mtg, UN Doc. GA/SHC/3729 (2002).

98 Marks, S., *supra* n.21, 150.

99 For example, United States President Bush stated at Monterrey that: 'The lesson of our time is clear. When nations close their markets, and opportunity is hoarded by a privileged few, no amount of development aid is ever enough.' International Conference on Financing for Development, Remarks by Mr. George W. Bush, President of the United States of America (Cintermex Convention Center, Monterrey, Mexico, 22 March 2002).

opposition to the right to development by defenders of the status quo indicates the right's potential value in altering an unjust system.

Consensus on the right to development was achieved in the Vienna Declaration and Programme of Action in 1993.[100] The political atmosphere created by the collapse of the Soviet Union and the scramble to attract capitalist investment eased the fears of developed states. The Vienna Declaration concludes that, 'the right to development, as established in the Declaration on the Right to Development, is a universal and inalienable right and an integral part of fundamental human rights'.[101] The Vienna Declaration displayed the commitment of the international community to cooperation to realize these rights.[102] Following this consensus, the Commission on Human Rights invited the Secretary General to organize global consultation with specialized agencies, non governmental organizations and states on the realization of the right to development.[103] The Global Consultation focused its report on practical problems such as integrating human rights standards into the operational activities of the United Nations system. It noted that development strategies based exclusively on economic and financial considerations failed to promote the right to development. [104]

At the time, a new trend in development discourse was evident. The focus had expanded to include human development.[105] This new aspect of development made it impossible to ignore human rights. Development practitioners appeared convinced that development strategies that ignore human rights are likely to fail. The agenda for one 1991 meeting of the United Nations Committee for Development Planning included a discussion of, 'the wide-spread trends towards democratization and participation, their relationship to poverty alleviation, and the role of international development efforts in supporting such trends'.[106] The right to development was now being discussed at a variety of levels within the United Nations system.

The right to development has since become an important aspect of the mandate of the High Commissioner for Human Rights.[107] The High Commissioner vowed to work towards establishing, 'a new branch whose primary responsibilities would include the promotion and protection of the right to development'.[108] The right has been regularly confirmed at international conferences and summits and in the

---

100   Vienna Declaration and Programme for Action, Articles 10 and 72.

101   *Ibid.* Article 10.

102   *Ibid.* Article 1.

103   Commission on Human Rights, 6 March 1989, Resolution 1989/45 based upon the recommendation of the Working Group in its last report, UN Doc. E/CN.4/1989/10, para.35. The General Assembly hoped this meeting would 'substantially contribute' to future implementation of the Declaration on the Right to Development, G.A. Res. 44/62 (1989).

104   The conclusions and recommendations of the meeting are found in UN Doc. E/CN.4/ 1990/9/Rev.1, Chapter 7.

105   Statement by Louise Arbour, *supra* n.5.

106   Committee for Development Planning, Report of the 26th Session, 3 Apr-4 May 1990, UN Doc. E/1990/27, para.49.

107   G.A. Res. 48/141, UN GAOR, 48th Sess., Supp. No. 49, UN Doc. A/48/141 (1993), para.261.

108   *Ibid.*, para.296.

annual resolutions of the General Assembly.[109] A consensus resolution on the right to development was reached when the Commission on Human Rights recommended to the Economic and Social Council the establishment of a follow-up mechanism consisting of an open-ended working group, and an Independent Expert on the subject.[110] Additionally, a large amount of academic work has been completed in support of the right to development.[111] The Independent Expert on the right to development has contributed a number of influential and supportive writings.[112] The commitment to the implementation of the right to development was overwhelmingly reaffirmed in the General Assembly in 2005.[113]

This evolution of the right to development to a prominent position in international development discourse has been confirmed for the new millennium. The heads of state and government gathered to address important concepts concerning the right to development. Led by developing states, the international community committed unequivocally to the right to development in the United Nations Millennium Declaration.[114] They asserted in article 11 that:

---

109   See General Assembly Resolutions: A/RES/59/185 (2005); A/RES/58/172 (2004); A/RES/57/223 (2003); A/RES/56/150 (2002); A/RES/55/108 (2001); A/RES/54/175 (2000); A/RES/53/155 (1999); A/RES/52/136 (1998); A/RES/51/99 (1997); A/RES/50/184 (1996); A/RES/49/183 (1995); A/RES/48/130 (1994); A/RES/47/123 (1992); A/RES/46/123 (1991); A/RES/45/97 (1990); A/RES/44/62 (1990); A/RES/43/127 (1988); A/RES/43/123 (1988); A/RES/42/117 (1987); A/RES/42/114 (1987); A/RES/41/98 (1986); A/RES/41/133 (1986); A/RES/41/132 (1986); A/RES/40/15 (1985).

110   Commission on Human Rights, 16 March-24 Apr 1998, Resolution 72, UN Doc. E/CN.4/1998/177, para.229.

111   See Mbaye, K. (1972), 'Le Droit du Développement comme un Droit de l'Homme, *Revue des Droits de l'Homme* 5, 503-34; Dupuy, R.-J. (ed.), *supra* n.65; Pellet, A. (1987), *Le Droit International du Développement* (2nd edn, Paris: Berger Levrault); Brownlie, I. (1989), *The Human Right to Development* (Commonwealth Secretariat Human Rights Unit Occasional Paper); Alston, P. (1988), 'Making Space for New Human Rights: The Case of the Right to Development', *Harvard Human Rights Year Book* 1, 3 and 20; Barsh, L., *supra* n.60, 322–38; Udombana, N. (2000), 'The Third World and the Right to Development: Agenda for the Next Millennium', *Human Rights Quarterly* 22, 753-87; Baxi, U. (1994), 'The Development of the Right to Development', in Baxi, U. (ed.), *Mambrino's Helmet?: Human Rights for a Changing World* (New Delhi: Har-Anand Publications, 1994), 22-32; Paul, J. (1992), 'The Human Right to Development: Its Meaning and Importance', *John Marshall Law Revue* 25, 235; Orford, A., *supra* n.9, 127; For a view against the right to development See Donnelly, J., *supra* n.11, 473.

112   Sengupta, A. (2000), 'Realizing the Right to Development', *Development and Change* 3.31, 553; Sengupta, A. (7 July 2001), 'Right to Development as a Human Right', *Economic and Policy Weekly*, 2527; Sengupta, A. (2002), 'Theory and Practice on the Right to Development', *Human Rights Quarterly* 24, 837; Sengupta, A. (2003), 'Development Co-operation and the Right to Development', in Morten Bergsmo (ed.), *Human Rights and Criminal Justice for the Downtrodden. Essays in Honour of Asbjørn Eide* (Leiden/Boston: Martinus Nijhoff).

113   G.A. Res. 59/185, 8 March 2005 (Yes: 181, No: 2, Abstentions: 4, Non-Voting: 4, Total voting membership: 191).

114   United Nations Millennium Declaration, Articles 11 and 24.

We will spare no effort to free our fellow men, women and children from the abject and dehumanizing conditions of extreme poverty, to which more than a billion of them are currently subjected. We are committed to making the right to development a reality for everyone and to freeing the entire human race from want.[115]

Article 24 of The Millennium Declaration states that the international community would 'spare no effort to promote democracy and strengthen the rule of law, as well as respect for all internationally recognized human rights and fundamental freedoms, including the right to development'.[116] The specific mention of the right to development in the Millennium Declaration is significant considering the apparent effort of the delegation to avoid rights-based language.[117]

The acceptance by the international community of the right to development continued at the United Nations Conference on Financing for Development in 2002. The Report of the International Conference on Financing for Development,[118] or the Monterrey Consensus, provides a blueprint of the new global approach to financing development. The Monterrey Consensus resolves to address the challenges of financing for development around the world. Their goals were set out in conjunction with the Millennium Declaration.[119] In its article 11, the Monterrey Consensus confirms the importance of the right to development as follows:

> Good governance is essential for sustainable development. Sound economic policies, solid democratic institutions responsive to the needs of the people and improved infrastructure are the basis for sustained economic growth, poverty eradication and employment creation. Freedom, peace and security, domestic stability, respect for human rights, including the right to development, and the rule of law, gender equality, market-oriented policies, and an overall commitment to just and democratic societies are also essential and mutually reinforcing.[120]

The outcome of this conference indicated an acceptance by the international community, including the most developed states, of the obligations surrounding the right to development including financial commitments. Developed states consistently avoid rights-based commitments and recoil from the implementation of the right to development. So why mention it in two important policy documents? Perhaps the answer lies in the general acceptance of neoliberal economic strategy and the embrace of globalization by developing states. Developed states may now assume that the revolutionary character of the right to development has been forgotten in the competition to attract foreign investment. Globalization is assumed to be permanently entrenched. Nevertheless, its reaffirmation in important international documents is

---

115   *Ibid.*, Article 11.
116   *Ibid.*, Article 24.
117   See Nelson, P. (2007), 'Human Rights, The Millennium Development Goals, and the Future of Development Cooperation', *World Development* 35.12.
118   The Report of the International Conference on Financing for Development, 18-22 March 2002, Monterrey, Mexico, UN Doc. A/CONF.198/11 (2002).
119   *Ibid.*, Preamble.
120   *Ibid.*, para.11.

vital for the right's legal development. Despite possible changed perceptions, the Declaration's rights-based content remains in tact.

The dialogue regarding the implementation of the international community's development goals is continuing. The follow up mechanism is now being discussed in the General Assembly's second High-level Dialogue on Financing for Development.[121] Furthermore, the Economic and Social Council held its special high-level meeting with the Bretton Woods institutions, the World Trade Organization and the United Nations Conference on Trade and Development on 18 April 2005, in which the overall theme was to provide coherence, coordination and cooperation for the implementation of the Monterrey Consensus and the Millennium Declaration.[122] The United Nations Third Conference on the Least Developed Countries insisted in this regard that, 'an enabling environment with peaceful solution of conflicts and respect for internationally recognized human rights, including the right to development, provides the best context for domestic and international resource mobilization'.[123] The process of implementation of the right to development is ongoing.

The Report of the Secretary General to the United Nations Economic and Social Council is very informative concerning the link between the Millennium Development Goals, the Monterrey Consensus and the right to development. In paragraph 7, the Report affirms:

> Another important link between the Millennium Development Goals and the conference outcomes is in the area of human rights. Although the Millennium Declaration reaffirmed the commitment to protect human rights, it is the World Conference on Human Rights that clearly postulated the indivisibility and inter-relatedness of democracy, development and human rights. That agreed human rights framework, including the right to development, provides a crucial foundation for the realization of the Millennium Development Goals. [124]

The report confirms that the right to development is also crucial to the process of democratization, the promotion of good governance and human rights. It clarifies that the human rights framework applicable to development includes the right to development. The report describes this framework as follows:

> The United Nations development agenda and Millennium Development Goals are based on a human rights framework as they follow from the Universal Declaration of Human Rights, the International Covenant on Civil and Political Rights, the International Covenant on Economic, Social and Cultural Rights; and the right to development. Human rights are also a requirement for reaching the Goals.[125]

---

121 High-level Dialogue on Financing for Development, UN Doc. A/59/PV.106 (2005).

122 'Towards achieving internationally agreed development goals, including those contained in the Millennium Declaration, Report of the Secretary General, UN Doc. E/2005/56 (2005).

123 Programme of Action for the Least Developed Countries, 2 July 2001, UN Doc. A/CONF.191/11, para.78.

124 *Ibid.*, Section II B (8), para.50.

125 *Ibid.*, Section II A (7).

The implementation of the international community's various developmental goals is a major focus of this report. The report confirms that the right to development is part of the Millennium Development Goals. It appears as though the final documents of the Millennium Summit and the Third United Nations Conference on the Least Developed Countries[126] have provided for indisputable obligations *vis-à-vis* the right to development.[127]

The fact that legal obligations for the right to development exist has been referred to by the International Monetary Fund. An International Monetary Fund representative stated to the Working Group on the right to development that the right to development process was different from the Poverty Reduction Strategy Papers initiative put forward by their organization.[128] The representative indicated that the International Monetary Fund's initiative, in contrast to the right to development, did not explicitly integrate human rights, have binding commitments or sanctions, or carry obligations beyond the articles of the Fund.[129]

The Report of the United Nations High Level Panel on Threats Challenges and Change builds on the outcome of the Millennium Summit.[130] It is a far reaching document that attempts to broaden the concept of collective security and link national interests with international cooperation. It does not explicitly mention the right to development. This is perhaps because in the interests of functionalism, the document is designed to appeal to powerful states and explain that development is in their interests. In doing so, it seeks to avoid previously politicized debates. Nevertheless, it emphasizes development as the 'indispensable foundation' of global security and stresses that failed development underlies many of the threats to security in the twenty first century.[131]

According to the High-Level Panel Report, this failure is due to a lack of preventative cooperation within the international community as, 'International institutions and states have not organized themselves to address the problems of development in a coherent, integrated way, and instead continue to treat poverty, infectious disease and environmental degradation as stand-alone threats.'[132] The Report of the High-Level Panel, in outlining what constitutes overcoming the 'challenge of prevention' directly links collective security with the achievement of the Millennium Development Goals and the Monterey Consensus.[133] Both of these indicators of international policy goals make explicit reference to the right to development as outlined above. Nevertheless, the failure to mention the right is a disappointing back track against rights-based development on the part of the United Nations.

---

126   Brussels Declaration, 2 July 2001, UN Doc. A/CONF.191/12.
127   E/CN.4/2002/28/Rev.1, *supra* n.12.
128   *Ibid.*
129   *Ibid.*
130   Report of the High-level Panel on Threats, Challenges and Change, UN Doc. A/59/564 (2004).
131   *Ibid.*, para.7.
132   *Ibid.,* para.55.
133   *Ibid.*, paras.59-65.

The then Secretary General of the United Nations, Kofi Annan, produced a further follow-up document to the Millennium Declaration entitled, 'In Larger Freedom'.[134] This document consolidated the outcomes of the major United Nations conferences and summits and advanced the concept of collective security and freedom based on international development. 'In Larger Freedom' acknowledges the historic opportunity available to the international community in 2005, citing unprecedented resources, technology and mechanisms for cooperation, to realize the right to development.[135] The 2005 World Summit Outcome recognized the importance of the right to development at the national level in terms of resource mobilization.[136] The document reaffirms that:

> ... good governance is essential for sustainable development; that sound economic policies, solid democratic institutions responsive to the needs of the people and improved infrastructure are the basis for sustained economic growth, poverty eradication and employment creation; and that freedom, peace and security, domestic stability, respect for human rights, including the right to development, the rule of law, gender equality and market-oriented policies and an overall commitment to just and democratic societies are also essential and mutually reinforcing.[137]

The World Summit Outcome also acknowledged the importance of human rights to international cooperation. It explained that the United Nations system needs to be strengthened, 'with the aim of ensuring effective enjoyment by all of all human rights and civil, political, economic, social and cultural rights, including the right to development'.[138] During the process that saw the Commission on Human Rights reformed as the Human Rights Council, the Secretary General stressed the importance of the right to development as part of a peer-review function, explaining that:

> ... its main task would be to evaluate the fulfillment by all states of all their human rights obligations. This would give concrete expression to the principle that human rights are universal and indivisible. Equal attention will have to be given to civil, political, economic, social and cultural rights, as well as the right to development.[139]

A series of open ended informal consultations on the new Human Rights Council put forward similar concerns. Many delegations referred to the 'importance of ensuring that economic, social and cultural rights as well as the right to development had the same importance and standing as civil and political rights in a new environment that should be defined against the background of the indivisibility and interrelatedness of

---

134 'In Larger Freedom: Towards Development, Security, and Human Rights for All', Report of the Secretary-General, UN Doc. A/59/2005 (2005).

135 *Ibid.*, para.27.

136 '2005 World Summit Outcome', UN Doc. A/Res/60/1 (2005).

137 *Ibid.*, para.24(b).

138 *Ibid.*, para.123.

139 'In larger freedom: Towards development, security, and human rights for all', *supra* n.134, Addendum: Human Rights Council, Explanatory Note by the Secretary General, para.6.

all human rights'.[140] The Office of the High Commissioner for Human Rights noted that the right to development must be put on an equal footing with other rights.[141] The Organization of the Islamic Conference also insisted that the right to development be within the new Council's mandate.[142]

These concerns about the right to development were addressed in the General Assembly Resolution Adopting the Human Rights Council which reaffirms, 'the commitment to strengthen the United Nations human rights machinery, with the aim of ensuring effective enjoyment by all of all human rights, civil, political, economic, social and cultural rights, including the right to development'.[143] It also stated that the work of the Human Rights Council would reflect the interdependence of all rights, including the right to development.[144]

The early work of the Human Rights Commission has reflected this emphasis on the right to development. In its first session, the Human Rights Council endorsed the conclusions and recommendations put forward by the Working Group on the Right to Development. Moreover, it renewed the mandate of the Working Group and decided to consider their next report at the 4th session.[145]

The Working Group envisions the right to development interacting with the Millennium Development Goals rather than being overshadowed by them. The Working Group has mandated a high level task force[146] to apply the right to development as a criterion for evaluating global development partnerships outlined in goal eight of the Millennium Development Goals.[147] The task force is charged with creating relevant criteria[148] and applying them to partnerships such as: The African Peer Review Mechanism,[149] The ECA/OECD-DAC Mutual Review of Development Effectiveness, The Paris Declaration on Aid Effectiveness and the Cotonou Partnership Agreement between European Union (EU) and African, Caribbean and Pacific (ACP) countries.[150] It is hoped that this will make the right to development relevant to current efforts at international development. Clearly this activity at the

---

140   Summary of the open-ended informal consultations held by the Commission on Human Rights pursuant to Economic and Social Council decision 2005/217, prepared by the Chairperson of the 61st session of the Commission, UN Doc. A/59/847-E/2005/73 (2005), para.18.

141   *Ibid.*, para.42.

142   *Ibid.*, para.68.

143   Human Rights Council, G.A. Res. 60/251, UN Doc. A/RES/60/251 (2006), Preamble.

144   *Ibid.*, para.4.

145   Human Rights Council, 'The Right to Development', Resolution 1/4, 2006.

146   Commission on Human Rights, 'The Right to Development', Resolution 2004/7, 2004, para.7.

147   Report of the high-level task force on the implementation of the right to development on its 4th session, A/HRC/8/WG.2/TF/2 (31 Jan 2008), para.3

148   Report of the Working Group on the Right to Development on its 8th session, A/HRC/4/47 (2007), para.54.

149   See 38th Ordinary Session of the Assembly of Heads of State and Government of the OAU: African Peer Review Mechanism AHG/235 (XXXVIII) (8 July 2002), Annex II.

150   For the initial results of this review see, A/HRC/8/WG.2/TF/2, *supra* n.147.

Human Rights Council signals the ongoing importance of the right to development. This initiative should be expanded to include the review of all agreements affecting development, including investment treaties.

The application of the right to development criterion in this manner has, 'provided the empirical basis for their progressive development and refinement'.[151] The Working Group wants to apply the right to development as an effective and practical tool for evaluation[152] and eventually lead to, 'the elaboration and implementation of a comprehensive and coherent set of standards',[153] based on 'actual practice'.[154] Developed states have begun to show their concern over collective responsibility by voting against recent resolutions at the general assembly.[155] This will result in pressure to dilute the radical components of the right to development. The danger with the Working Group's current approach is that through consultation with member states, development partners and agencies, the international responsibility component of the right to development will be reduced in order to generate broader consensus.

Nevertheless, this activity further indicates the importance the international community places on the right to development. If implemented, it would help ensure the realization of other rights in a climate dominated by economic globalization. In this context Espiell notes that solidarity rights are, 'a prerequisite for the existence and exercise of all human rights'.[156]

The Rights-based Content of the Right to Development

The content of the right to development must be clarified. The developed world's legal opposition to the right to development formally stems from the imprecise nature of the Declaration's content, which it claims is vague and inconsistent.[157] The United States leads the opposition to the legal obligations of the right to development, insisting that, 'We cannot support the call to make progress on realizing the right to development. There is no internationally accepted definition of such a right. Making such a call is premature and irrelevant.'[158] Yet, a thorough reading of the Declaration

---

151   A/HRC/4/47, *supra* n.148, paras.49 and 54.

152   *Ibid.*, para.51.

153   *Ibid.*, para.52.

154   *Ibid.*, para.55.

155   A recent General Assembly Draft Resolution on the Right to Development (A/RES/61/169, 2007) was adopted by 134 votes to 53. The 53 opponents were all developed or states with immediate financial connections to developed states.

156   Gross Espiell, H., *supra* n.15, 1168.

157   Alston cited this as a strength of the document and commented that it allowed for evolution, Alston, P., *supra* n.48, 221.

158   Statement by Joel Danies, U.S. Representative to the UN Human Rights Commission, Summary Record of the 63rd Meeting, 59th Sess, UN Doc., E/CN.4/2003/SR.63 (2003), paras.5 and 15.

on the Right to Development accompanied by various explanations by academic experts[159] and the independent expert[160] provides a reasonable definition.

Opposition to the right to development is politically motivated. Many human rights provisions are, or have been, difficult to translate directly into a precise binding legal context. International instruments result from diplomatic discourse, which means compromise, often creating vague and possibly inconsistent resolutions and declarations. The Declaration on the Right to Development is no more vague than certain provisions of investment protection agreements that states so readily endorse.

There is now a work in progress to clarify the options for implementation of the right to development and to discuss binding legal standards, guidelines and principles stemming from the Declaration.[161] The right to development is formulated in a sparing manner, but that the vagueness does not deprive it of meaning. Consensus is difficult as this document remains politically controversial. Perhaps a parsimonious approach is beneficial in that it encourages participation by the most states and then allows for progressive development of standards.

Donnelly suggests that there is a tendency to treat the right to development as a synthesis of more traditional human rights.[162] Critics worry that this might work to undermine campaigns for established human rights by placing them all under a misinterpreted concept governed by a non-binding convention. Ghai notes that specific rights pertaining to such areas as speech, assembly and social welfare are in danger of being overlooked in favour of a conceptual right to development that remains clear only to progressive human rights scholars.[163] Alston counters that this criticism of the right to development is similar to that directed at all rights of solidarity.[164] The failure of states to faithfully implement already agreed upon human rights during development necessitates international responsibility. Orford explains that, 'No state can use the Declaration as authority for the argument that other rights can be put on hold or violated while development is achieved.'[165]

The need to define the content and obligations arising from the right to development resulted in the consensus establishment of the Open-Ended Working Group and the Independent Expert by the Commission in 1998.[166] This initiative was designed to study the current state of the implementation of the right to development and discuss

---

159   See Barsh, L., *supra* n.60; Baxi, U., *supra* n.111; Ansbach, T. et al. (1992), *The Right to Development in International Law* (Leiden and Boston: Martinus Nijhoff); Orford, A., *supra* n.9.

160   See Sengupta, A. (2003), *supra* n.112.

161   Commission on Human Rights, 'The Right to Development', Resolution 2003/83, UN Doc. E/CN.4/RES/2003/83; for the most recent work see, A/HRC/8/WG.2/TF/2, *supra* n.147.

162   Donnelly, J., *supra* n.11, 481.

163   Gai, Y. (1994), 'Human Rights and Governance: The Asia Debate', *Australian Year Book of International Law* 15, 10.

164   Alston, P., *supra* n.45, 316.

165   Orford, A., *supra* n.9, 140.

166   Commission on Human Rights, Report on its 54th Session, Resolution 72, UN Doc. E/CN.4/1998/177 (1998), para.229.

concepts raised through this process.[167] The result has been a move towards a binding legal standard based on the Declaration,[168] opposed by many developed States.[169] Opposition insists that the right to development is a national priority and that there should be no legal obligation for members of the international community.[170]

In response, the Independent Expert has insisted that the right to development represents a composite right to a process of development.[171] The broad and indistinct scope of the process outlined by the Declaration should be viewed in a positive light, as it allows for adaptation to dynamic international economic, political and cultural circumstances. The Declaration on the Right to Development is deferential to international law principles of self-determination, non-interference and territorial sovereignty.[172] Therefore there is no precise outline of development. That is left for states to decide in a participatory and equitable manner.[173] A violation of any human rights caused by development policy indicates a violation of the right to development process.[174]

The primary content of the right to development is the rights-based approach. The purpose of the right to development is to empower people in a process of development that constitutes more than economic growth. It puts forward a system in which legal safeguards against inequality and for entitlements are ensured through accountability mechanisms. The right to development recognizes the challenges facing developing states and calls upon the international community to assist them. To realize a rights-based development in the context of globalization requires a process blueprint such as the Declaration.[175]

Defining Development: The Rights-based Approach

The content of the Declaration on the Right to Development is rights-based. The rights-based approach gained credence following the failures of the structural adjustment era. It has extended from use in community activism to international

---

167   *Ibid.*, para.233.

168   Resolution 2003/83, *supra* n.161.

169   Marks, S., *supra* n.18, 140; for a detailed outline of the legal evolution on the right to development see Lindroos, A., *supra* n.1, 3-7.

170   Report of the Secretary General on the Right to Development, UN Doc. A/58/276 (2003), para.11.

171   Sengupta, A., *supra* n.10, 853.

172   On these fundamental legal principles guiding international relations see, Cassese, A. (2001), *International Law* (Oxford University Press), 86-112.

173   Sengupta, A., *supra* n.10, 853. States have the right to determine development priorities as long as they conform to human rights law, ICCPR, Article 1; International Covenant on Economic, Social and Cultural Rights (adopted 16 Dec 1996, entered into force 3 Jan 1976), G.A. Res. 2200A (XXI), 21 UN GAOR Supp. No. 16 at 49, UN Doc. A/6316 (1966), 993 U.N.T.S. 3 (ICESCR), Article 1; DRD, Article 1.

174   Fifth Report of the Independent Expert on the Right to Development, UN Doc. E/CN.4/2002/WG.18/6 (2002), paras.5 and 6.

175   E/CN.4/2002/28/Rev.1, *supra* n.12., para.38.

and national development policy.[176] Proponents argue that the rights-based approach can 'lend moral legitimacy and the principle of social justice' to development.[177] Nonetheless, the precise definition and application of the term remains elusive. The rights-based approach has been criticized, like the Millennium development goals as legitimizing donor activities through the rhetorical inclusion of human rights language.[178]

Development can mean different things to different people and states may not prioritize human rights. The rights-based approach helps qualify and legitimize development initiatives considered to promote the right to development. Human development indicators, such as the provision of food, health, education and employment, have augmented gross domestic product as indicators of development. The rights-based approach converts these indicators into rights and entitlements.[179] This approach should strengthen rather than replace governance by identifying rights holders and duty bearers.[180] It insists that needs are regarded as legal entitlements and on an institutional process of participation, empowerment, non-discrimination and accountability. The rights-based approach has proven useful in empowering local civil society, combating the root causes of poverty such as inequality and discrimination as well as qualifying development initiatives by promoting accountability.[181]

The rights-based approach stresses the indivisible and interdependent nature of all human rights entitlements within a process. Instrumental freedoms bring about constitutive rights. Participatory rights are instrumental.[182] Sen argues that, 'Greater freedom enhances the ability of people to help themselves and also to influence the world.'[183] Without the instrumental rights, the constitutive economic, social and cultural rights cannot be achieved. Without constitutive rights, instrumental freedoms have little meaning. In this manner, rights are both the ends and means of development.[184] There are stand-alone constitutive freedoms that are essential factors of the human development process. Human rights form both the process and the goals essential in the process of development. The right to development is meant as the instrumental guideline to the process of achieving its constituents.

---

176   See Darrow, M. and Tomas, A. (2005), 'Power, capture, and conflict: a call for human rights accountability in development cooperation', *Human Rights Quarterly* 27.2, 471–538; Nelson, P. and Dorsey, E. (2003), 'At the nexus of human rights and development: new methods and strategies of global NGOs', *World Development* 31, 2013–26.

177   United Nations Development Programme (UNDP) (2000), *Human Development Report 2000* (New York: Oxford University Press), 3.

178   Uvin, P., *supra* n.22, 2.

179   United Nations Development Programme (UNDP) (2002), *Human Development Report 2002: Deepening Democracy in a Fragmented World* (New York: Oxford University Press), 22.

180   *Ibid.*, 23.

181   For a study on empowerment through a rights-based approach see, Nelson P., *supra* n.117.

182   *Ibid.*, 38.

183   Sen, A. (1999), *Development as Freedom* (Oxford University Press), 18.

184   *Ibid.*, 40.

The rights-based approach as elucidated by the Office of the High Commissioner for Human Rights similarly puts forward five tenets. These are: links to human rights law, participation, equality, non-discrimination and accountability.[185] The United Nations High Commissioner for Human Rights, Louise Arbour, has confirmed that the right to development requires the rights-based approach. In her statement to the Working Group on the Right to Development, she noted that:

> ... there has to be an enabling environment – legal, political, economic and social-sensitive and reflective of the local context for the realization of the right to development. The creation of such an environment hinges critically on the respective motivations of states – individually and collectively – to apply, observe and adjudicate, in the process of development, the human rights standards and the principles of participation, accountability, non-discrimination, equality, empowerment and cooperation.[186]

These principles are advocated for both normative and instrumental reasons. The normative is driven by the legal and morally intrinsic value of human rights linked to obligations entailed by the United Nations Charter and other core human rights norms. Instrumental value is motivated by a need for more effective development planning in addressing issues now linked to human rights. Human rights norms address social exclusion, promote empowerment, reinforce participatory systems and strengthen accountability mechanisms.[187] Without a mechanism to deal with inequitable power relations, development can be reduced to a set of state goals or aspirations.

The rights-based approach requires policies and obligations that are all legally accountable. The language of human rights, based on binding international legal obligations, provides the tools and references for development policy. Thus, participation, empowerment, non-discrimination and accountability become implicit in development projects as rights of people.

However, the rights-based approach is not strictly a legal one. It is concerned with social change and uses law insofar as it is able to promote this change. Despite its importance, law is weakened in the context of asymmetrical power relations where it can be distorted or ignored with impunity.[188] Human rights need to apply in diverse situations not limited to courts and tribunals.[189] Accountability is available through other mechanisms such as monitoring, reporting, public debate and citizen participation. Universal human rights norms agreed upon by consent strengthen rationality and objectivity in development policy making. This can promote human development as well as economic development.

---

185 United Nations Office of the High Commissioner for Human Rights (OHCHR), 'Human Rights in Development: Rights-based Approaches' (available online: <www.unhchr.ch/development/approaches-04.html>, accessed 18 March 2008).

186 Statement by Louise Arbour, *supra* n.5.

187 Darrow, M. and Tomas, A., *supra* n.176, 492.

188 Ibid., 487.

189 Moser, C. et al. (2001), 'To Claim Our Rights: Livelihood, Security, Human Rights and Sustainable Development' (Overseas Development Institute, published online: <www.odi.org.uk/rights/Publications/tcor.pdf>, accessed 18 March 2008), 21-25.

The rights-based approach is not part of a static process. The right to development demands incremental application.[190] The rights-based approach should guide the formulation of policies, laws and strategy as well as influencing budgetary, judicial, educational and political decisions.[191] It is a process in which strategy is devised in a participatory manner to suit local developmental requirements rather than a top down dictation by experts applying a uniform strategy.[192]

The Declaration on the Right to Development commits states to establish an order conducive to the realization of human rights law. The Declaration refers to a rights-based process.[193] States have the primary responsibility for development, individually and as members of the international community. But many states are limited by global economic processes. Therefore, the international dimension is an important factor in assisting states to promote and protect human rights at the national level.[194] The rights-based approach is essential to ensure that national level policy making considers human rights and keeps the ownership of the right to development in people's hands. The rights-based approach has been granted considerable support from the international community and has been accepted as a part of the process in achieving the right to development.[195] The important contribution of the rights-based approach is to elevate human rights on par with the interests of corporations in globalization/development at the national level.

Expressed Linkage to Human Rights Law   Development discourse has not traditionally been based on, or linked directly to, human rights law. This link is vital as it codifies the relationship between development and human rights law, recognizing the need for economic growth as well as the other responsibilities of

190   E/CN.4/2004/23/ADD.1, *supra* n.24, para.18(1).

191   United Nations Development Programme (UNDP) (2002), Workshop on the Implementation of a Rights-based Approach to Development: Training Manual (available online <www.undp.org/governance/cd/documents/713.pdf.>, accessed 18 March 2008), 6-7 and 149.

192   For example see, United Nations Children's Fund (UNICEF), Regional Office South Asia (SARO) (2000), *Saving Women's Lives: A Call to Rights-based Action*.

193   Sengupta, A., *supra* n. 10, 846; 'The Human Rights-based Approach to Development Cooperation: Towards a Common Understanding Among the UN Agencies', *Report: The Second Interagency Workshop on Implementing a Human Rights-based Approach in the Context of UN Reform* (Stamford, Connecticut, 5–7 May, 2003) available at: <www.mrforum.se/upload/files/2/R%C3%A4ttighetsperspektivet/Common%20Understanding%20FN%202003.pdf.>, accessed 18 March 2008), 17.

194   E/CN.4/2002/28/Rev.1, *supra* n.12., para.40.

195   Many development agencies have acknowledged support for the rights-based approach to development. For example See UNDP (2000), *supra* n.177; The United Kingdom Department for International Development (2000), 'Realizing Human Rights for Poor People' (published online <www.dfid.gov.uk/pubs/files/tsphuman.pdf>, accessed 18 March 2008); The Swedish International Development Agency (SIDA) (2001), 'Working Together: The Human Rights-based Approach to Development Cooperation' (Stockholm Workshop, 16–19, October 2000, published online <www.ihmisoikeusliitto.fi/julkaisut/hrbad/fredriksson.pdf>, accessed 18 March 2008).

states.[196] The rights-based approach attempts to integrate human rights law and development discourse. Alston notes that human rights offer the following to development discourse:

1. a solid basis for values and policy choices that otherwise are more readily negotiable
2. a predictable framework for action, with the advantage of objectivity, determinacy, and the definition of appropriate legal limits
3. a quintessentially empowering strategy for the achievement of human centred goals
4. a ready legal means to secure redress for violations
5. a secure basis for accountability, not only for the state party concerned, but also for a significantly wider range of actors in international development cooperation.[197]

All development objectives must be defined in human rights terms as the first step in a rights-based approach. This transforms development discourse from needs and charity to legal entitlements and legal obligations based upon human rights law. There is no explicit mention of development aid in the Declaration on the Right to Development.[198] The Declaration, instead, calls for obligations on the part of the international community to be responsible for ensuring an environment conducive to the realization of human rights.[199] This promotes entitlements and obligations rather than needs and charity.

The formulation of development policy in terms of rights and entitlements instead of needs and goals is vital for empowerment. Goals are utilitarian in nature, defining an aspiration to maximize welfare gains.[200] On the other hand, rights claim that all people are entitled to dignity, certain kinds of treatment and to protection from others. Rights apply to groups and individuals while goals apply to states and donors. Therefore, the application of human rights, from a perspective of social change and human development, is preferable to setting out goals.

The elimination of human rights from development discourse removes a potential catalyst for political and social change. Human rights provide a foundation of non-discrimination from which to build a society of equality. Underdevelopment is often caused by injustices that human rights law is designed to confront. Without this confrontation, development can be dictated from above and is more likely to reflect the interests of powerful states and actors such as the corporation. For example, in the international financial institution's Poverty Reduction Strategy Papers, states volunteer to set out goals and work with donors to improve development indicators.[201]

196   Sano, H.-O. (2000), 'Development and Human Rights: The Necessary, but Partial Integration of Human Rights and Development', *Human Rights Quarterly* 22, 735.

197   Alston, P. (1998), 'What's in a Name: Does it Really Matter if Development Policies Refer to Goals, Ideals or Human Rights?' in Helmich, H. and Borghese, E. (eds), *Human Rights in Development Cooperation* (OECD Development Centre, Netherlands Institute of Human Rights), 105-106.

198   Lindroos, A., *supra* n.1, 42.

199   DRD, Articles 1(1),5 and 7.

200   Nelson P., *supra* n.117, 2045.

201   See International Monetary Fund (2005), 'Poverty Reduction Strategy Papers (PRSPs)' (available online <http://www.imf.org/external/np/exr/facts/prsp.htm>, accessed 18 March 2008).

Likewise, the Millennium Development Goals commit states to reducing egregious development failures through trade and aid.[202]

According to the Declaration on the Right to Development, development initiatives must focus on the interdependence of all human rights.[203] This linkage necessitates consideration of the Covenant on Economic, Social and Cultural Rights, which includes international obligations for states and international agencies in a position to provide assistance.[204] The rights-based approach to development can help civil society ensure good national programming practices and effective implementation.[205]

Participation and Empowerment   Linking human rights discourse to development policy can only succeed in conjunction with popular participation. Development policy must be applied in a specific context in consultation with local groups ensuring that human rights law guides development. The Declaration on the Right to Development is founded upon the principles of participation. Its preamble states that, 'development is a comprehensive economic, social, cultural and political process, which aims at the constant improvement of the well-being of the entire population and of all individuals on the basis of their active, free and meaningful participation in development and in the fair distribution of benefits resulting there from'. This provides authoritative guidance on participation parameters within development programmes.[206]

Human rights-based development requires meaningful participation. Participation has been described as, 'the right through which all other rights in the Declaration on the Right to Development are exercised and protected'.[207] The right to development must be a continuing participatory process at the local, regional, national, and international levels.

Participation rights are firmly grounded in human rights standards. Although participation during development is a multidisciplinary practice, human rights law provides a vital checklist.[208] The International Bill of Rights guarantees the right to take part in government and public affairs with access to public services.[209] The Human Rights Committee determined that the conduct of public affairs covers all aspects of public administration, including the formulation of policy at the international,

---

202   See United Nations Millennium Declaration, Goal 8, which calls for creating a global partnership for development, envisions a coherent set of aid, trade and financial institutions and arrangements. Interestingly, Goal 8 includes international responsibilities but does not include benchmarks or deadlines.

203   DRD, Article 6(2).

204   ICESCR, Article 2.

205   'The Human Rights-based Approach to Development Cooperation', *supra* n.193.

206   Darrow, M. and Tomas, A., *supra* n.176, 509.

207   Report on the Global Consultation on the Realization of the Right to Development as a Human Right, *supra* n.42, para.48.

208   Darrow, M. and Tomas, A., *supra* n.176, 507.

209   UDHR, Article 21; ICCPR, Article 25(a).

national, regional and local levels.[210] Participation rights are also included in the Convention on the Rights of the Child and the Convention on the Elimination of All Forms of Discrimination against Women and the Convention on the Elimination of All Forms of Racial Discrimination.[211]

The widespread, applied, and specific use of the rights-based approach is more and more linked to social movement campaigns, which adds an important political dimension.[212] For example, the fight against HIV/AIDS has seen NGOs and social movements advocate for broader access to essential medicines. Advocacy against states for the right to HIV/AIDS treatment has appealed to human rights law in countering corporate power.[213] The Treatment Action Campaign's (TAC) strategies in South Africa provide examples of how a rights-based approach can empower local civil society in order to enact lasting social change.[214] It is this type of action that makes states prefer development goals rather than development rights.

Goals encourage states to go for quick fix strategies rather than a long term approach of addressing the structural inequalities at the heart of underdevelopment.[215] The right to development calls for states to tackle the causes of underdevelopment instead of addressing its symptoms. It empowers civil society to challenge government failures and ensure human rights in the local context.

There are clear instrumental advantages to a participatory and inclusive development system. It can utilize local knowledge, expose local preferences, raise efficiency and allocation of resources, and maximize the ownership and sustainability of the development process.[216] Pledging a consultation process is only the first step towards empowerment through participation in development. Active roles must be assumed by domestic populations in order to fulfill the requirements of a participatory right.[217] A rights-based approach calls attention to the quality of participation, in contrast to superficial measures such as imported quick fix technical

---

210   Human Rights Commission, 'The right to participate in public affairs, voting rights and the right of equal access to public service (Article 25)', General Comment 25, UN ESCOR, 57th Sess., 1510th mtg., 5, UN Doc. CCPR/C/21/Rev.1/Add.7 (1996).

211   Convention on the Rights of the Child, adopted 20 Nov 1989, entered into force 2 Sept 1990, G.A. Res. 44/25, annex, 44 UN GAOR Supp. (No. 49) at 167, UN Doc. A/44/49 (1989) (CRC), Article 12; Convention on the Elimination of All Forms of Discrimination against Women, adopted 18 Dec 1979, entered into force 3 Sept 1981, G.A. Res. 34/180, 34 UN GAOR Supp. No. 46 at 193, UN Doc. A/34/46 (CEDAW) Article 7, 13 and 14(2); International Convention on the Elimination of All forms of Racial Discrimination, adopted 21 Dec 1965, entered into force 4 Jan 1969, G.A. Res. 2106 (XX), Annex, 20 U.N. GAOR Supp. (No. 14) at 47, U.N. Doc. A/6014 (1966), 660 U.N.T.S. 195 (ICERD), Article 5.

212   Nelson P., *supra* n.117, 2044.

213   *Ibid.*

214   See Friedman, S. and Mottiar, S. (2005), 'A Rewarding Engagement: The Treatment Action Campaign and the Politics of HIV/AIDS' *Politics and Society* 33, 511-65.

215   Nelson P., *supra* n.117, 2046.

216   See Osami, S. (2000), *Participatory Governance, Peoples Empowerment and Poverty Reduction*, United Nations Development Programme, Social Development and Poverty Division Conference Paper Series No. 7 (New York: Oxfam).

217   Ginther, K. (1992), 'Participation and Accountability: Two Aspects of the International Dimension of the Right to Development', *Third World Legal Studies* 57.

systems.[218] 'Participation in a human rights sense means having the power to exercise authoritative influence over the development process, rather than simply being consulted about pre-determined results', writes Orford.[219] According to the Declaration on the Right to Development, the state should encourage popular participation.[220]

While participation is now widely recognized by most developmental agencies, it is often misinterpreted. Participation often results in no more than a consultation process in which local communities are convinced of the merits of projects already decided upon.[221] The aim of participation must be ownership of the development process. Partnership rather than stewardship breeds empowerment. Partnership must afford participants a capacity to analyze, negotiate and alter power relations.[222] The African Charter for Popular Participation in Development and Transformation emphasizes the important connection between participation and empowerment in development as follows:

> ... the role of the people and their popular organizations is central to the realization of popular participation. They have to be fully involved, committed and, indeed, seize the initiative. In this regard, it is essential that they establish independent people's organizations at various levels that are genuinely grass-root, voluntary, democratically administered and self-reliant and that are rooted in the tradition and culture of the society so as to ensure community empowerment and self-development. Consultative machinery at various levels should be established with governments on various aspects of democratic participation. It is crucial that the people and their popular organizations should develop links across national borders to promote co-operation and interrelationships on sub regional, regional, South-South and South-North bases. This is necessary for sharing lessons of experience, developing people's solidarity and rising political consciousness on democratic participation.[223]

Empowerment requires participation in the planning, policy formulation, project design, allocation of resources, as well as the implementation and distribution of costs and benefits of development projects. It must be characterized by an ability to influence political and economic agendas, more than as a consumer of public

---

218   Darrow, M. and Tomas, A., *supra* n.176, 506.

219   Orford, A., *supra* n.9, 139.

220   DRD, Article 8(2).

221   Alston, P., *supra* n.48, 235.

222   VeneKlasen, L. et al. (2004), *Rights-based Approaches and Beyond: Challenges of Linking Rights and Participation* (Institute of Development Studies, Working Paper No. 235), 5 (available online <www.ids.ac.uk/ids/bookshop/wp/wp235.pdf.>, accessed 18 March 2008).

223   African Charter for Popular Participation in Development and Transformation, Resolution 691 (XXV), adopted at the 25th session of the Commission and 16th meeting of the Economic Commission for Africa Conference of Ministers responsible for Economic Planning and Development at its 267th meeting on 19 May 1990, contained in Report of the Economic and Social Council. Development and International Cooperation, UN Doc. A/45/427 (1990), para.11.

services.[224] The World Bank defines empowerment as, 'the expansion of assets and capabilities of poor people to participate in, negotiate with, influence, control and hold accountable institutions that affect their lives'.[225]

The empowerment process must be guaranteed at the local, regional, national and international level, as part of a comprehensive system.[226] It is suggested that with reference to participation and empowerment, 'the Declaration on the Right to Development fleshes out further normative content for programmatic purposes, notwithstanding lack of consensus on the Declaration's international legal status'.[227] De Feyter observes that in a time of economic globalization this need for popular participation is more acute as decisions are taken with little local involvement.[228]

Non-discrimination and Fair Distribution   Discrimination based on race, religion and gender is contrary to customary international law.[229] This fundamental norm of human rights law is based on articles 55 and 56 of the United Nations Charter, articles 2 and 7 of the Universal Declaration of Human Rights, the International Covenants on Human Rights,[230] and state practice.[231] Article 6.1 of the Declaration emphasizes participation and empowerment as the foundation for development without discrimination. It declares that, 'All states should co-operate with a view to promoting, encouraging and strengthening universal respect for and observance of all human rights and fundamental freedoms for all without any distinction as to race, sex, language or religion.'[232]

Human rights-based approaches to development trace the social, economic, political, and other causes of rights deprivation to patterns of discrimination in law, institutions, and policy. The rights-based approach emphasizes the need to

---

224   Orford, A. and Beard, J. (1998), 'Making the State Safe for the Market: The World Bank's World Development Report 1997', *Melbourne University Law Review* 22, 209–10.

225   World Bank (20029, *Empowerment and Poverty Reduction: A Sourcebook*, 14.

226   Lindroos, A., *supra* n.1, 46; UNICEF, supra n.192, 32-45.

227   Darrow, M. and Tomas, A., *supra* n.176, 507 (n.98).

228   De Feyter, K. (2006), 'Discussion Paper: Localizing Human Rights' (Antwerp: Institute of Development Policy and Management).

229   See Dissenting Opinion of Judge Tanaka in the South West Africa cases, ICJ Reports, 1966,3, 293; 37 ILR,243, 455; Shaw, M. (2003), *International Law* (5th edn, Cambridge University Press), 266-67; Simma, B. and Alston, P. (1988-89), 'The Sources of International Law: Custom, Jus Cogens, and General Principles', *Australian Year Book of International Law* 12, 82.

230   ICESCR, Article 2.2; ICCPR, Article 2.1.

231   See ICERD; Declaration on Race and Racial Prejudice (1982), UN Doc. E/CN.4/Sub.2/1982/2/Add.1, annex V; Declaration on the Elimination of All Forms of Intolerance and of Discrimination Based on Religion or Belief (1981), G.A. Res. 36/55, 36 UN GAOR Supp. No. 51 at 171, UN Doc. A/36/684, 1981; Declaration on the Rights of Persons Belonging to National or Ethnic, Religious or Linguistic Minorities (1993), G.A. Res. 47/135, annex, 47 UN GAOR Supp. No. 49 at 210, UN Doc. A/47/49; World Conference Against Racism, Racial Discrimination, Xenophobia and Related Intolerance, Programme of Action, Agenda item 9, adopted 8 Sept 2001, Durban South Africa, UN Doc. A/CONF.189/5.

232   DRD, Article 6(1).

establish effective legal and institutional protections for groups that are subject to discriminatory treatment.[233]

The rights-based approach requires the incorporation of safeguards to protect against threats to vulnerable groups. All decisions must seek to empower these groups and address existing power imbalances. Examples of such imbalances include relations between land owners and peasants, men and women, as well as workers and employers.[234] Objective equality requires redressing these relations, for example, in the form of affirmative action programmes.[235] Many civil society groups utilize a rights-based approach in this manner to tackle discrimination in development that is overlooked in top down goal orientated policy.[236]

The current development paradigm has been plagued by inequitable distribution and unfair access to the proceeds of globalization. Resource distribution claims based on equality and human dignity are prominent in the Declaration.[237] Article 8 instructs that states should 'ensure equality of opportunity for all in their access to basic resources, education, health services, food, housing employment and the fair distribution of income'. Furthermore, article 8 provides that, 'appropriate economic and social reforms should be carried out with a view to eradicating all social injustices'. This denotes the importance of the role of the state in promoting and protecting human rights through redistribution programmes.[238]

Article 2(3) of the Declaration explicates that states have both the right and the duty to formulate appropriate national development policies that aim at the fair distribution of the benefits of economic development. This right and duty implies that outside actors should not prevent states from fulfilling their duties. This would seem to include developed states who negotiate investment agreements and corporations that utilize them to reduce the regulatory role of developing states.

Accountability   The rights-based approach hinges on accountability, without which, its other elements become voluntary initiatives subject to economic considerations. Participation, empowerment and non-discrimination are clearly linked to the accountability of decision makers.[239] Civil and political rights, such as free press, access to information, and freedom of association, should guarantee

---

233   Nowak, M. (2002), 'A Human Rights Approach to Poverty', *Human Rights in Development Yearbook 2002: Empowerment, Participation, Accountability and Non-discrimination: Operationalising a Human Rights-based Approach to Development* (Leiden: Martinus Nijhoff Publishers), 28-29.

234   Darrow, M. and Tomas, A., *supra* n.176, 505.

235   Human Rights Commission (1989), General Comment on Non-Discrimination, General Comment No. 18, UN. GAOR, 37th Session, addendum 8, 10, UN Doc. CCPR/C/21?Rev.1/Add.1.

236   See Picard, M. (2004), 'Measurement and Methodological Challenges to CARE International's Rights-based Programming (2004), *Enterprise Impact News* 33.

237   DRD, Preamble, Articles 2(2) and 8(1); see also, Sano, H.-O., *supra* n.196, 741.

238   Lindroos, A., *supra* n.1, 47.

239   Department for International Development (2004), *Strategies for Achieving International Development Targets: Realizing Human Rights for Poor People* (DFID), 24.

a legal framework.[240] Accountability is promoted by identifying rights holders and their entitlements and matching them with duty bearers under human rights law.[241] The rights-based approach focuses on empowering rights holders in relation to duty bearers. This requires states to do more than reach goals. They must fulfill their role as protectors of human rights law by ensuring that non-state actors do not violate human rights.[242]

The point is to move beyond shaming corporations and pressuring governments. The rights-based approach encourages implementation of international norms in local law. This accountability can assist civil society in to create social change and address unequal power relations. Under a rights-based approach, states have the primary obligation for the realization of human rights.[243] They must strengthen the role of parliaments, human rights institutions, and an independent media in order to successfully implement a rights-based development programme.[244]

Human rights standards should establish stronger accountability through periodic reporting to the treaty bodies who have limited authority to mount investigations and publicize reports condemning violators. However, human rights suffers from a lack of accountability. The development of national laws, policies and institutions coupled with redress mechanisms are essential for accountability. Existing judicial remedies may be inadequate and require legislative, community-based, and informal mechanisms to supplement them.

The Declaration on the Right to Development does not directly address accountability but it has featured in related policy and programme activity.[245] Many rights require a process of fulfillment. They can be realized only if the appropriate policies are adopted over time.[246] Therefore states must retain their ability to enact policy. The right to development should entitle people to demand policy in line

---

240   *Ibid.*

241   United Nations Development Programme (UNDP) (2000), *Human Development Report: Human Rights and Human Development* (UNDP), 24-26.

242   'The Human Rights-based Approach to Development Cooperation', *supra* n.143.

243   See, Economic Social and Cultural Rights Commission, 'The Nature of States Parties' Obligations', General Comment 3, UN ESCOR, 5th Sess. 11, UN Doc. E/1991/23, annex III, para.86.

244   Darrow, M. and Tomas, A., *supra* n.176, 513.

245   See ECOSOC Official Records, UN Doc. E/CN.4/1334 (1979); The International Dimensions of Development as a Human Right', Report of the Secretary General, UN Doc. ST/HR/Ser.A/8; Seminar on the Effects of the Existing Unjust International Economic Order on the Economies of the Developing Countries and the Obstacles That This Represents for the Implementation of Human Rights and Fundamental Freedoms, Geneva, 30 June-11 July 1980, UN Doc. ST/HR/SER.A/10; Seminar on the Relations that Exist Between Human Rights, Peace and Development, UN Headquarters, New York, 3-14 August 1981, UN Doc. E/1979/36, Supplement No. 6; Report on the 35th Session of the United Nations Commission on Human Rights, UN Doc. E/1982/12 Supplement No. 2. Current efforts of the Working Group on the Right to Development and the High Level Task Force are now focusing on methods to hold states accountable, see, A/HRC/8/WG.2/TF/2, *supra* n.147.

246   Sen, A. (1984), 'The Right Not to Be Hungry', Alston, P. and Tomasevski, K. (eds), *The Right to Food* (Kluwer Accademic), 70.

with that process.[247] This most likely requires a binding agreement that can ensure compliance between many actors with differing agendas.[248]

Accountability requires an open process of progressively implementing human rights. Although civil and political rights are not subject to progressive realization and must be fulfilled immediately, many important aspects of the right to development require the provision of economic, social and cultural rights. Article 2.1 of the Covenant on Economic, Social and Cultural rights obligates states to, 'take steps ... with a view to achieving progressively the full realization of the rights recognized in the present Covenant'. The Committee on Economic, Social and Cultural Rights clarifies this obligation as follows:

> ... it is on the one hand a necessary flexibility device, reflecting the realities of the real world and the difficulties involved for any country in ensuring full realization of economic, social and cultural rights. On the other hand, the phrase must be read in the light of the overall objective, indeed the raison d'être, of the Covenant which is to establish clear obligations for states parties in respect of the full realization of the rights in question. It thus imposes an obligation to move as expeditiously and effectively as possible towards that goal.[249]

This acknowledges that certain rights will not be achieved in the short run but must be accomplished incrementally over time. The Declaration on the Right to Development similarly stresses that, 'Steps should be taken to ensure the full exercise and progressive enhancement of the right to development, including the formulation, adoption and implementation of policy, legislative and other measures at the national and international levels.'[250]

Accountability must include the principle of non-retrogression. 'Any deliberately retrogressive measures ... would require the most careful consideration and would need to be fully justified by reference to the totality of the rights provided for in the Covenant and in the context of the full use of the maximum available resources', cautions the Committee on Economic Social and Cultural Rights.[251] The principle of non-retrogression requires states strive to continually improve human rights during development. A minimum core standard for all rights must be maintained. Failure to ensure nutrition, healthcare, education or housing, subject to resource constraints, indicates a violation.[252]

Human rights law sets universal standards while imposing legal obligations.[253] In recognition of the right to development as a human right, the international community has accepted its responsibility for the realization of this process. The

---

247　*Ibid.*
248　Sengupta, A., *supra* n. 10, 844.
249　Committee on Economic, Social and Cultural Rights (1991), General Comment Number 3: The nature of States parties obligations (Article 2, para.1 of the Covenant), UN Doc. E/1991/23, para.9.
250　DRD, Article 10.
251　UN Doc. E/1991/23, *supra* n.249, para.9.
252　*Ibid.*, para.10.
253　Sengupta, A., *supra* n. 10, 845.

process outlined in the Declaration sets an agenda in which norms are established for peoples, the state and the international community for achieving a rights-based development. This is in contrast to aspirational development goals decided upon between donors, corporations and states.

Rights-based Approach and 'Elite Capture'

The rights-based approach's emphasis on empowerment, equality and accountability can help to control the phenomena of elite capture in the development process. The rights-based framework of accountability prevents unilateral decision making. The right to development is often misconstrued as denoting economic growth alone and reflecting corporate interests. The rights-based approach is ignored as the right becomes a state's right to economic growth. It is then argued that it requires market reform in order to be realized.[254]

Elites put forward that the state's only development responsibility should be to facilitate economic growth. A statement of the International Chamber of Commerce provides an example: 'Realization of the right to development is heavily depended upon the vitality of the private business sector. In order for states to fulfill society's right to development, they must do much more to foster the growth, expansion, and productivity of businesses.' [255] Thus, development is reduced to terms of gross domestic product.[256] Orford explains that:

> It has become accepted by many states and some commentators that the right to development is a right of states to pursue a narrow economic model of development over the human rights of the people of the state invoking the right. The right to development is presented as allowing states where necessary to put the interests of investors over the interests of other human beings. While the right to Declaration on the Right to Development does not provide all the answers to that problem, it certainly offers a different interpretation of the right.[257]

Although the economic growth strategy may provide resources for the right to development,[258] dependency theorists argue that underdevelopment is necessary in an international capitalist system based on economic growth alone.[259] Moreover,

---

254   Orford, A., *supra* n.9, -45.

255   The Sub-Commission's Draft Norms, If Put into Effect, Will Undermine Human Rights, the Business Sector of Society, and the Right to Development, Joint Views of the International Organization of Employers and the International Chamber of Commerce on the Draft Norms on the Responsibilities of Transnational Corporations and other Business Enterprises with Regard to Human Rights, 34 (available online <www.reports-and-materials. org/IOE-ICC-views-UN-norms-March-2004.doc.>, accessed 19 March 2008).

256   See Roxborough, I. (1979), *Theories of Underdevelopment* (London: Macmillan).

257   Orford, A., *supra* n.9, 144.

258   Sen, A., *supra* n.183, 111.

259   See Gunder Franck, A. (1975), *On Capitalist Underdevelopment* (Oxford University Press); Cardoso, H. and Faletto, E. (1979), *Dependency and Development in Latin America* (The University of California Press); Jameson, K. and Wilbur, C. (eds) (1996), *The Political Economy of Development and Underdevelopment* (6th edn, New York: McGraw-Hill).

markets foster efficiency, and profits rather than social equality.[260] This is not sufficient for rights-based development.[261] Market-based development does not address inequality.[262] Elites in developed and developing states may collude in order to advance their own interests.[263]

Globalization has not substantially altered the number of people living in poverty.[264] The gap between the richest and poorest states as well as the concentration of wealth within states has grown,[265] resulting in increased inequality between and within states.[266] Inequality fosters an environment in which the proceeds of growth are 'captured' by elites contrary to the right to development.[267] Darrow and Tomas explain that:

> Inequality breeds inequality, facilitating a disproportionate capture of the benefits of growth by the 'haves,' including in situations where functioning democratic institutions exist. Naturally, income is not the only relevant issue in this context. Public policies in fundamental areas such as education and health often neglect the poor and favour the wealthy, with potentially far reaching consequences for the achievement of human dignity and well being.[268]

Exclusive focus on economic growth to the detriment of human rights is contrary to the rights-based approach. Elite capture of the development process entrenches economic exploitation. Indigenous groups or minority rights can be pushed aside to make way for economic development projects. This circumvention of rights is not uncommon as states prioritize investment interests over all human rights.[269] The Declaration on the Right to Development reflects an attempt to prevent this.

National and international accountability mechanisms are lacking and contribute to inequality.[270] This reflects the disempowerment of the majority of poor people.[271] These people cannot wait for the benefits of market-based strategies to trickle down from the elites.[272] Participation, empowerment and accountability must become

---

260   Donnelly, J. (1999), 'Human Rights, Democracy and Development', *Human Rights Quarterly* 21.3, 628.

261   Sen, A., *supra* n.183, 118.

262   *Ibid.*, 119.

263   James, P. (1997), 'Postdependency? The Third World in an Era of Globalization and Late Capitalism', *Alternatives* 22, 205.

264   The Human Development Report explains that improvement was driven by China's economic growth while he rest of the world's poverty numbers remained unchanged or worsened. (UNDP) (2002), *supra* n.179, 18.

265   See Davies, J. et al. (2006), 'World Distribution of Household Wealth' (World Institute for Development Economics Research of the United Nations University UNU-WIDER).

266   Darrow, M. and Tomas, A., *supra* n.176, 474.

267   UNDP, *supra* n.179, 46-47.

268   Darrow, M. and Tomas, A., *supra* n.176, 475.

269   Orford, A., *supra* n.9, 143.

270   UNDP, *supra* n.179, 2.

271   Darrow, M. and Tomas, A., *supra* n.176, 475.

272   Stiglitz, J., *supra* n.21, 78-80.

components of development strategy. These qualities help to rectify the asymmetries of power and 'elite capture' that plague development strategies.[273]

The rights-based approach is a political and legal imperative that engages with accountability deficits. It seeks to overcome development limitations by confronting power relations. The human rights-based approach treats power relations as central to the development process. Otherwise, the entitlements of the poor can be manipulated by the wealthy.[274] The rights-based approach sets legal limits to decision making by elites and provides minimal guarantees to the disadvantaged.

This approach focuses on policy making choices for states, rather than allowing only for reaction to markets. Linking development discourse to human rights law identifies national and international legal obligations that delimit development choices to ones that promote, secure and protect human rights. A rights-based approach can help to ensure sustainable long-term growth built upon a human rights foundation. This requires states to retain the ability to formulate rights-based development policy. The Declaration on the Right to Development envisions a very different agenda from the process put forward by the international community based on growth alone.[275]

Rights of solidarity still raise contention as their duties and mechanisms for implementation remain 'skeletal' and unclear.[276] Many questions linger concerning their implementation, especially in an era of declining sovereignty for developing states and of 'powerful and influential multinational corporations'.[277] Nevertheless, the regional bodies have enforced these skeletal rights of solidarity, for example the right to a healthy environment by the African Commission[278] and the Inter-American Commission.[279]

These bodies have progressively defined the content of the right to an environment by linking it with other more established international law. Importantly, these regional systems have dealt directly with the role of states in protecting these rights from the actions of corporations. This shows that even in the early days of third generation rights jurisprudence, action can be taken. The right to development should evolve along similar lines in the future.

---

273   Darrow, M. and Tomas, A., *supra* n.176, 472.

274   *Ibid.*, 489.

275   Eide, A. (1989), 'Realization of Economic, Social and Cultural Rights and the Minimum Threshold Approach', *Human Rights Law Journal* 10.1-2, 35.

276   Aginam, O. (2000), 'Two Sides of a Coin – Human Rights and Multinational Investment in Africa: The Case of Nigeria', *Africa Legal Aid Quarterly* 25.

277   *Ibid.*, 23.

278   See, *Social and Economic Rights Action Center for Economic and Social Rights v. Nigeria*, African Commission on Human and Peoples' Rights, Comm. No. 155/96 (2001) at 50-65.

279   For example see, Inter-American Commission on Human Rights, Resolution No. 12/85, Case No. 7615 (Brazil), 5 March 1985, printed in Annual Report of the Inter American Commission on Human Rights 1984-85, OEA/Ser.L/V/II.66, Doc. 10, Rev. 1, 1 Oct 1985, at 24, 31(YANOMAMI CASE).

Duties Arising From the Right to Development

Human rights in development require correlated duties of States.[280] Rights must be defined in terms of obligations and responsibility for their realization. However, human rights in a globalized world do not consist of perfect obligations.[281] Instead, rights must be fulfilled not just by the state, but by other actors of the international community capable of contributing.[282] The relationship between the rights holder and duty bearer is not always direct, as much depends on the international community. Now, the state not only must protect, promote and fulfill human rights at the national level; it must also ensure act at the international level.

In a world of imperfect obligations, a plan of action, or process, is required for the realization of human rights.[283] The right to development is this process.[284] The Declaration's preamble affirms this view explaining that, 'development is a comprehensive economic, social, cultural and political process, which aims at the constant improvement of the well-being of the entire population and of all individuals on the basis of their active, free and meaningful participation in development and in the fair distribution of benefits resulting there from'.[285]

The Declaration on the Right to Development sets forth a process that contains corresponding domestic and international rights and duties for the state in conjunction with the international community.[286] The legal process outlined in the content of the Declaration prioritizes human rights over aspirations for economic growth and the expansion of global investment.[287] This process must be coordinated with the international community's acceptance of its responsibilities within the international economic, political and legal structure, or by changing the structure if necessary.[288]

This process consists of a set of rights-based policies sequentially consistent with a phased realization of the desired outcomes.[289] When a process is given the status of an inalienable human right, the means (the rights-based process) become as important as the ends (human development). The legal process has been described by Sengupta as a vector in which each element is a human right along with the vector itself.[290] In order to promote this vector, rights must improve while none can be violated. This is a continuous process which requires the interdependent enjoyment

---

280   Sen, A., *supra* n.183, 227-31.
281   Sengupta, A., *supra* n. 10, 843.
282   Sen, A., *supra* n.183, 227-31.
283   *Ibid.*, 230.
284   The Working Group on the Right to Development explains that the right to development is a process of development in which 'all human rights and fundamental freedoms can be fully realized'. Working Group on the Right to Development, Review of progress and obstacles in the promotion, implementation, operationalization, and enjoyment of the right to development, UN Doc. E/CN.4/2004/WG.18/2, para.3.
285   DRD, Preamble.
286   E/CN.4/2002/28/Rev.1, *supra* n.12., para.40.
287   *Ibid.*, para.38.
288   Sengupta, A., *supra* n. 10, 843.
289   *Ibid.*, 870.
290   *Ibid.*